O HOLY NIGHT

O HOLY NIGHT

IDEALS PUBLICATIONS INCORPORATED
NASHVILLE, TENNESSEE

ISBN 0-8249-4179-9

Printed and bound in the U.S.A. by R.R. Donnelly & Sons, Willard, Ohio.

Library of Congress Cataloging-in-Publication Data
O holy night / editor, Julie K. Hogan
     p. cm.
   Includes index.
   ISBN 0-8249-4179-9 (alk. paper)
   1. Jesus Christ--Nativity--Literary collections. 2. Christmas--Literary
   collections. 3. Christian literature. I. Hogan, Julie, 1949-
PN6071. J4 O15 1999
808.8'0351--dc21
                                 99-048355
                                  CIP

10 8 6 4 2 1 3 5 7 9

Editor and Compiler, Julie K. Hogan
Research Assistant, Mary Dunn

Publisher, Patricia A. Pingry
Designer, Eve DeGrie
Associate Editor, Thorunn McCoy
Copy Editor, Elizabeth Kea

Color Film Separations by Precision Color Graphics,
Franklin, Wisconsin.

Published by Ideals Publications Incorporated
535 Metroplex Drive, Suite 250
Nashville, TN 37211

All Scripture references taken from the
King James Version of the Bible.

Cover: THE HOLY NIGHT by Feuerstein/ H. Armstrong Roberts

ACKNOWLEDGMENTS

Achtemeier, Paul and Elizabeth. Excerpt from THE OLD TESTAMENT ROOTS OF OUR FAITH by Paul and Elizabeth Achtemeier. Reprinted by permission of the authors. Andersen, Jean Jones. "The Innkeeper" from ENCOUNTERS AT BETHLEHEM by Jean Jones Andersen, © 1985 by Jean Jones Andersen. Buck, Pearl S. and Lyle Kenyon Engel. "A Prayer is Answered" from THE STORY BIBLE. Reprinted by permission of Harold Ober Associates Incorporated, copyright 1971 by Pearl S. Buck and Lyle Kenyon Engel. Burgess, Anthony. Excerpt from MAN OF NAZARETH by Anthony Burgess, copyright 1979. Reprinted by permission of McGraw Hill. Coatsworth, Elizabeth Jane. "Twelfth Night: Song of the Camels." Published by arrangement with the Estate of Louis Untermeyer, Norma Anchin Untermeyer c/o Professional Publishing Services Company. This permission is expressly granted by Laurence S. Untermeyer. Daniel-Rops, Henry. From JESUS AND HIS TIMES by Henri Daniel-Rops, trans. by Ruth Millar, copyright 1954, 1956 by E.P. Dutton. Used by permission of Dutton, a division of Penguin Putnam Inc. Dickinson, Emily. "The Saviour must have been." Reprinted by permission of the publishers and the Trustees of Amherst College from THE POEMS OF EMILY DICKINSON, Ralph W. Franklin, ed., Cambridge, Mass.: The Belknap Press of Harvard University Press, Copyright © 1998, by the President and Fellows of Harvard College. Copyright © 1951, 1955, 1979 by the President and Fellows of Harvard College. (ACKNOWLEDGMENTS CONTINUE ON PAGE 160)

(ACKNOWLEDGMENTS CONTINUE ON PAGE 160)

CONTENTS

THE PROMISE OF HOPE

O Holy Night, the stars are
brightly shining;
It is the night of the dear
Saviour's birth.

PROMISES OF HOPE

or unto us a child is born, unto us a son is given: and the government shall be upon his shoulder: and his name shall be called Wonderful, Counsellor, The mighty God, The everlasting Father, The Prince of Peace.

Of the increase of his government and peace there shall be no end, upon the throne of David, and upon his kingdom, to order it, and to establish it with judgment and with justice from henceforth even for ever. The zeal of the Lord of hosts will perform this (*Isaiah 9:6–7*).

Behold, the days come, saith the LORD, that I will perform that good thing which I have promised unto the house of Israel and to the house of Judah. In those days, and at that time, will I cause the Branch of righteousness to grow up unto David; and he shall execute judgement and righteousness in the land (*Jeremiah 33.14–15*).

But thou, Bethlehem Ephratah, though thou be little among the thousands of Judah, yet out of thee shall he come forth unto me that is to be ruler in Israel; whose goings forth have been from of old, from everlasting (*Micah 5:2*).

Then shall we know, if we follow on to know the Lord: his going forth is prepared as the morning; and he shall come unto us as the rain, as the latter and former rain unto the earth (*Hosea 6:3*).

Abraham and Isaac are listed in the ancestry of Jesus, the King of kings, whose birth was announced by the angels. In Gaudenzio Ferrari's painting ABRAHAM AND THE THREE ANGELS *(SuperStock) the angels also announce to Abraham that his wife, Sarah, will bear him a child. This child, Isaac, fulfilled God's promise that Abraham would be the "father of many nations" and that "kings shall come out of thee."*

AND A LITTLE CHILD SHALL LEAD THEM

nd there shall come forth a rod out of the stem of Jesse, and a Branch shall grow out of his roots:

And the spirit of the LORD shall rest upon Him, the spirit of wisdom and understanding, the spirit of counsel and might, the spirit of knowledge and of the fear of the LORD;

And shall make Him of quick understanding in the fear of the LORD:

And righteousness shall be the girdle of his loins, and faithfulness the girdle of his reins.

The wolf also shall dwell with the lamb, and the leopard shall lie down with the kid; and the calf and the young lion and the fatling together; and a little child shall lead them. And the cow and the bear shall feed; their young ones shall lie down together: and the lion shall eat straw like the ox (*Isaiah 11:1–3, 5–7*).

Edward Hicks's illustration of Isaiah 11:5-7 captures THE PEACEABLE KINGDOM *(Art Resource, NY), the harmony of all earthly life that the Messiah will bring.*

GOD ANNOUNCES HIS PLANS

FULTON J. SHEEN

istory is full of men who have claimed that they came from God or that they were gods or that they bore messages from God.

Reason dictates that if any one of these men actually came from God, the least thing that God could do to support His claim would be to pre-announce His coming.

If God sent anyone from Himself or if He came Himself with a vitally important message for all men, it would seem reasonable that He would first let men know when His messenger was coming, where He would be born, where He would live, the doctrine He would teach, the enemies He would make, the program He would adopt for the future, and the manner of His death. By the extent to which the messenger conformed with these announcements, one could judge the validity of his claims.

It is true that the prophecies of the Old Testament can be best understood in the light of their fulfillment. The language of prophecy does not have the exactness of mathematics. Yet if one searches out the various Messianic currents in the Old Testament and compares the resulting picture with the life and work of Christ, can one doubt that the ancient predictions point to Jesus and the kingdom which He established: God's promise to the patriarchs that through them all the nations of the earth would be blessed; the prediction that the tribe of Judah would be supreme among the other Hebrew tribes; the strange yet undeniable fact that in the Bible one finds the virgin birth of the Messiah clearly predicted; the prophecy of Isaiah about the patient sufferer, the Servant of the Lord, who will lay down His life as an offering for His people's offenses; and the perspectives of the kingdom of the House of David. In whom but Christ have these prophecies found their fulfillment?

A SPOTLESS ROSE

A spotless Rose is blowing,
Sprung from a tender root
Of ancient seers' foreshowing,
Of Jesse's promised fruit;
Its fairest bud unfolds to light

Amid the cold, cold winter
And in the dark midnight.
The Rose which I am singing,
Whereof Isaiah said,
Is from its sweet root springing

In Mary, purest maid;
For through our God's great
    love and might,
The blessed Babe she bare us
In a cold winter's night.

AUTHOR UNKNOWN

Jesus may have walked beneath a date palm tree similar to this one as He taught along the shores of the Sea of Galilee. Photo of date palm tree by Lior Rubin.

THAT HOLY THING

They all were looking for a king
To slay their foes and lift them high:
Thou cam'st, a little baby thing
That made a woman cry.

O Son of Man, to right my lot
Naught but Thy presence can avail;
Yet on the road Thy wheels are not,
Nor on the sea Thy sail!

My how or when Thou wilt not heed,
But come down Thine own secret
   stair,
That Thou mayst all my need—
Yea, every bygone prayer, answer all
   my need—
Yea, every bygone prayer.

    George MacDonald

Jesus lived and taught in the rolling hills around the Sea of Galilee. Using landmarks and scenes familiar to the fishermen and farmers who lived in the area, Jesus' early ministry was aimed at the people living in the towns surrounding this freshwater lake. In His parables, mustard seeds, fishing, and farming are all mentioned. Photo of the Sea of Galilee taken from the Mount of Beatitudes by Thomas R. Fletcher.

HOW IT ALL BEGAN

Morton Kelsey

ur ever-surprising Creator knew the depth and potential of the creatures that had been created. God also knew that human beings are far more touched and convinced by pictures, images, and stories than they are by abstractions, concepts, ideas, and logic. In the small province of Palestine in the reign of Herod, God staged the greatest drama ever presented. God was the producer, the lead actor, and the prompter, and God even provided an audience. Divine providence carefully prepared a time and place in history and selected just the right characters for the divine drama. God's mysterious play was acted on a huge stage before the entire ancient world.

The cast, stage properties, and plot twists were numerous. They included Mary, Joseph, and the baby Jesus; Zacharias, Elisabeth and John the Baptist; Caesar Augustus and his imperial taxation decree; the forced trip to Bethlehem and the donkey who carried Mary; the shepherds and the angels that appeared to them; the innkeeper; the stable; the Magi and their star; Herod and his court and soldiers; the dreams through which the Spirit and the angels spoke to many of the characters; the priests at the circumcision and Mary's purification; Anna; Simeon; the slaughtered children; the extras who were the people in Nazareth and the crowds in Jerusalem and Cairo. The scene shifts from Nazareth to Rome, from Bethlehem and Jerusalem to Egypt, and then back to Nazareth.

ROYAL DAVID'S CITY

JENNY ROBERTS

he first mention of Bethlehem, the birthplace of Christ, is in the book of Genesis, for it was nearby that Rachel, Jacob's wife, died giving birth to her son, Benjamin, and was buried. The town is referred to both by its older name of Ephratah and as Bethlehem. It was sometimes called Bethlehem Ephratah or Bethlehem Judah, to distinguish it from another Bethlehem that lay northwest of Nazareth.

Bethlehem also appears in the Old Testament book of Ruth. A family from Bethlehem traveled to Moab to escape famine in Judah. The widowed Naomi returned to her homeland, accompanied by her Moabite daughter-in-law, Ruth, who refused to leave her and vowed to adopt Naomi's religion and people as her own. When they returned to Bethlehem, Ruth worked as a reaper in the fields of Naomi's rich kinsman, Boaz, who eventually married her. Ruth and Boaz were the great-grandparents of David.

Ruth's descendants remained in Bethlehem, for when the prophet Samuel was sent to anoint a king over Israel to be Saul's successor, God told him to choose one of the sons of Jesse the Bethlehemite, Ruth's grandson. Samuel traveled to Bethlehem where God directed him to choose David, the youngest son, a boy who spent his days looking after his father's sheep in the hills outside Bethlehem. After David became king, Bethlehem became a Philistine garrison town. Although David reigned as king in Jerusalem, which was known as "the City of David," Bethlehem established a vital claim to that title as the place of David's birth and boyhood.

The last mention of Bethlehem in the Old Testament comes from Micah, who prophesies, "But thou, O Bethlehem Ephratah . . . out of thee shall he come forth unto me that is to be ruler in Israel" (5:2). This prophecy is repeated at Christ's birth in the Gospel of Matthew.

JUST WHERE I AM

The stars are lovely things
    at night;
They light the hills and
    make them bright.
They lift the valley
    from its knees
And make the plains
    as bright as these.

One star shines brighter
    than the rest;
It is the one I like the best.
It marks the place
    of Jesus' birth,
Of angel song
    and peace on earth.

Were I a shepherd, I
    would go
Down in the valley
    far below
And worship
    at a manger stall
In Bethlehem,
    the Lord of all.

Were I a wise man from afar,
I, too, would follow that
    bright star;
But, as I only am a lamb,
I kneel to Him
    just where I am.

MINNIE KLEMME

God spoke through the prophet Micah and announced that the Messiah would be born in Bethlehem, a small town in the province of Judah. Today Jesus' birthplace has grown into a bustling city. Photo of Bethlehem by Richard T. Nowitz.

COME, O LONG EXPECTED JESUS

Come, O long expected Jesus,
Born to set Your people free;
From our fears and sins release us;
Free us from captivity.

Israel's strength and consolation,
You, the hope of all the earth,
Dear desire of ev'ry nation,
Come, and save us by Your birth.

Born Your people to deliver;
Born a child and yet a king!
Born to reign in us forever
Now Your gracious kingdom bring.

By Your own eternal Spirit
Rule in all our hearts alone;
By Your all sufficient merit
Raise us to Your glorious throne.

CHARLES WESLEY

The terraced fields outside Bethlehem look much as they did when Joseph and Mary traveled to the city. Olive trees and grapevines are still grown on the hillsides. Photo of terraced fields by Betty Crowell.

THE PLACE OF THE NATIVITY

JENNY ROBERTS

 The story of Jesus' birth in Bethlehem is told in just two of the Gospels, Matthew and Luke. The Gospel of Luke tells the familiar story of Mary and Joseph traveling from Nazareth to Bethlehem in order to be "enrolled"— that is, registered and taxed.

Bethlehem was not an obscure village at the time of Jesus' birth, as it is often represented. It was near the busy main road from Jerusalem to Gaza via Hebron and much visited by travelers. It was also close to the site of the Herodium, a conical hill where Herod had built a combined fortress and pleasure palace with a swimming pool and formal gardens.

In some ways the town has hardly altered over the centuries. In the hills around the town, nomadic Arabs set up their tents and shepherds watch their flocks, like the boy David and also the shepherds of the Christmas story. The approach to Bethlehem is along a dusty road lined with stone terraces planted mainly with olive trees. The traveler's first view of the town is of flat-roofed white houses clustered together on a hillside. Many old houses in the town are built over caves cut into the limestone. The caves are level with the road, and a flight of rough steps leads up to the one-room houses where the family lives. The caves, housing animals and mangers, or stone troughs, are often cut into the rock. It was probably in just such a cave that Jesus was born.

JESUS' WORLD

Bread was the main staple of the Hebrew diet. To make the bread, wheat or barley was ground into a coarse flour, which was then combined with water and leavening from saved day-old dough. Women fashioned the dough into round, flat loaves and baked them.

Jesus, who called Himself the "bread of life" (*John 6:48*) was born in Bethlehem, a name that means "city of bread."

The Bible uses bread as a metaphor for all food, but Jesus used the word as a metaphor for spiritual nourishment as well. Jesus said, "I am the bread of life; he that cometh to me shall never hunger" (*John 6:35*).

Mary and Joseph traveled to Bethlehem to register for the census. Under Roman rule, Israel's population was almost two million people. Half were Jewish; the remaining were Romans, Greeks, Egyptians, Syrians, and Persians.

The cities of Bethlehem and Jerusalem are located in the province of Judah. The city of Nazareth is located in the province of Galilee.

Sheep were central to the sustenance and wealth of the Hebrew people. They provided food and clothing and also served as a sacrifice in religous rituals. The Bible often refers to Jesus as the "lamb of God" because of His sacrifice. Photo of sheep in hills of Israel by Lior Rubin.

The daily meal mainly consisted of breads, fruits, and vegetables. The fertile fields in Judah produced lettuce, onions, beans, lentils, grapes, figs, dates, and pomegranates. During the time of Christ, people ate meat rarely, usually for special occasions.

Matthew traces the lineage of Jesus back to Abraham. Luke traces Jesus' family tree to Adam.

During the time of Christ, potters made cooking-pots, jars, and tableware. They also fashioned small lamps out of the same type of clay.

These earthenware pots date to the time of Christ and were used to hold olive oil. Oil is mentioned over two hundred times in the Bible and was important in cooking, commerce, medicine, and occasions such as the anointing of kings. Photo by Jeff Greenberg/ New England Stock.

Women spun flax and wool, then wove and dyed the fabrics; these were then made into garments for their families. Both men and women wore tunics under loose, hooded outer garments; the men's were knee-length, and the women's were ankle-length.

Shoe leather came from sheep or goats. All but the very poor wore sandals perhaps similar to the ones pictured above. Photo by Victor Englebert.

At the time of Jesus, a person's status could be determined by his or her clothes. The poor wore wool; the rich wore silk. Purple garments were a sign of wealth since purple dye was made from mollusks found in the Mediterranean Sea.

AND HIS NAME SHALL BE CALLED WONDERFUL

"His name shall be Wonderful." This Babe for whom,
Even in village inns, there was no room?

The lowing of cattle was His lullaby,
Though caroling angels were thronging the sky.

"His name shall be Wonderful." This Carpenter,
Known from His childhood by each villager?

"His name shall be Wonderful." Spat upon, shamed,
Tortured and crucified—how is He named

Wonderful, Counselor, Mighty God,
He who one dark day Golgotha's road trod?

His name shall be Wonderful—Jesus, God's Son!
God's Word has promised, and it shall be done!

Not meek and lowly, despised among men,
This same Lord Jesus is coming again

With clouds and great glory, to reign here below,
And all men shall praise Him, and each knee shall bow.

From ocean to ocean His name shall be heard,
Wonderful name of our wonderful Lord!

MARTHA SNELL NICHOLSON

Jesus, who was foretold by the prophet Isaiah as the Prince of Peace, was known to many as the carpenter's son. The town of Nazareth, Jesus' boyhood home, is located in the northern section of Judah. When He began His ministry, Jesus moved closer to the Sea of Galilee. There He called the apostles, Andrew and Simon, to leave their fishing nets and become "fishers of men." Later, Jesus calmed the stormy sea and walked upon its waters. Photo of the Sea of Galilee by Nik Wheeler.

THE FULFILLMENT OF GOD'S PROMISE

PAUL AND ELIZABETH ACHTEMEIER

Through every book of the New Testament, the fulfillment in Christ can be traced. He is the new Israel and the new Messiah upon whom the spirit of God is poured out. He is the descendant of David, ruling over a universal kingdom. He is the Messiah of peace, bringing justice, righteousness, and faithfulness to His people in the strength of the Lord. In infinite detail, the New Testament proclaims that He is the One expected; on page after page, it testifies that God has kept His solemn promise.

Perhaps first and foremost, however, we should understand Jesus Christ as the fulfillment of the obedient Son. Through the course of the Gospels we can trace His obedience: His refusal in His desert temptations to serve any other ruler but God, His rejection of even the closest human ties as more important than His relationship with His heavenly Father, His total subjection of man's life with man to God's will and purpose for the community, His constant refusal in His dealings with the scribes and Pharisees to conform to merely human standards of morality and religion. In every deed and word, Jesus acknowledged the sole lordship of God until His obedience brought Him finally to a dark garden called Gethsemane, where in sorrow and agony, He sweated out His final surrender, "Father, if thou art willing, remove this cup from me; nevertheless not my will, but thine, be done" (Luke 22:42).

Here was the true Son of God. Here was the descendant of Abraham and of David who perfectly followed His heavenly Father. Here was the new Israel, the One of unshakable faith. Here was the obedient Israel whom God could use for His purpose.

The land along the Sea of Galilee is some of the most fertile land in all of Israel. Wheat and barley are easily grown in the rich soil. Photo of farmland along the Sea of Galilee by Alan and Sandy Carey.

O COME, O COME, EMMANUEL

O come, O come, Emmanuel,
And ransom captive Israel,
That mourns in lonely
    exile here,
Until the Son of God appears.

O come, Thou Rod of Jesse, free
Thine own from Satan's tyranny.
From depths of hell Thy
    people save
And give them vict'ry o'er
    the grave.

O come, O Dayspring, come
    and cheer
Our spirits by Thine advent here
And drive away the shade
    of night
And pierce the clouds and bring
    us light.

Rejoice! Rejoice! Emmanuel
Shall come to thee, O Israel.

ISAAC WATTS

In 1947 a Bedouin boy was searching for a lost goat among the mountains surrounding the Dead Sea. In a cave the boy made a surprising discovery: large earthen jars containing leather scrolls wrapped in linen. The best preserved of these Dead Sea scrolls contains the entire manuscript of the book of Isaiah. The words of Isaiah contain numerous passages describing the coming of the Messiah. Photo of the mountains surrounding the Dead Sea by Nik Wheeler.

A NAME OF HOPE

WOLFGANG TRILLING

The prophet Isaiah announced, "Behold, a virgin shall conceive." The mysterious circumstances which had filled Joseph with dismay are not so disturbingly new. The virgin birth wrought by the Spirit was already intimated in the Old Testament. The eyes of faith recognize the action of God across the centuries and know how to understand the promises in light of their fulfillment.

There is something else in the prophecy: a name which is just as profound and rich as the name "Jesus," "Emmanuel," or "God with us." The knowledge that Yahweh was always with His people was something deeply ingrained in the faith of Israel. It was Israel's distinction and its glory. The prophets proclaim: "Fear not: for I have redeemed thee; I have called thee by thy name; thou art mine. When thou passest through the waters, I will be with thee; and through rivers, they shall not overflow thee. When thou walkest through the fire, thou shalt not be burned; neither shall the flame kindle upon thee" (Isaiah 43:1–2).

During the years of captivity there remained the hope that God would be with His people in the future. It was a fact, and yet it was a promise. They could experience the presence of God, but still they had to wait for it. The manner of God's future presence to His people, which remained to be realized, was clearly to be something quite new.

And now it seems to have become reality. The Child who is to be born bears the name which is the full description of this hope: "God with us." The nearness of God given here is, therefore, not to be made manifest in any thing or place, but in a man whose nature it is to be God with us. In Him and through Him God is near and present more closely and more really than ever before.

THE WAY IS PREPARED

Long lay the world in sin and
error pining, till He appeared
and the soul felt its worth.

THE ANGEL GABRIEL APPEARS TO ZACHARIAS

here was in the days of Herod, the king of Judaea, a certain priest named Zacharias, of the course of Abia: and his wife was of the daughters of Aaron, and her name was Elisabeth. And they were both righteous before God, walking in all the commandments and ordinances of the Lord blameless. And they had no child, because that Elisabeth was barren, and they both were now well stricken in years. And it came to pass that while he executed the priest's office before God in the order of his course, according to the custom of the priest's office, his lot was to burn incense when he went into the temple of the Lord.

And there appeared unto him an angel of the Lord standing on the right side of the altar of incense. And when Zacharias saw him, he was troubled, and fear fell upon him. But the angel said unto him, Fear not, Zacharias: for thy prayer is heard, and thy wife Elisabeth shall bear thee a son, and thou shalt call his name John. And thou shalt have joy and gladness; and many shall rejoice at his birth. For he shall be great in the sight of the Lord.

And Zacharias said unto the angel, Whereby shall I know this? For I am an old man and my wife well stricken in years.

And the angel answering said unto him, I am Gabriel, that stand in the presence of God; and am sent to speak unto thee, and to show thee these glad tidings. And, behold, thou shalt be dumb, and not able to speak, until the day that these things shall be performed, because thou believest not my words, which shall be fulfilled in their season.

And the people waited for Zacharias, and marvelled that he tarried so long in the temple. And when he came out, he could not speak unto them: and they perceived that he had seen a vision in the temple: for he beckoned unto them, and remained speechless (*Luke 1: 5–9, 11–15, 18–22*).

The angel Gabriel appears as a messenger and an interpreter. In the Old Testament, Gabriel helps Daniel interpret the vision of the ram and the goat. The Master of Avignon's THE GUARDIAN ANGEL *(SuperStock) captures God's angelic messenger.*

A PRAYER IS ANSWERED

PEARL S. BUCK AND LYLE KENYON ENGEL

acharias was full of wonderment. "How can this be?" he asked. "How shall I know that this is true? For my wife and I are old, too old to have a child."

The angel answered, "I am Gabriel, who stands in the presence of God. The Lord has sent me to you to tell you these glad tidings. But because you do not believe my words, which nevertheless will be fulfilled when the right time comes, you shall be dumb and not able to speak until the day that these things shall be performed. Let that be your sign that what I say is true."

Zacharias looked again but the angel was no longer there. The people in the temple court waited for the priest, wondering why he stayed so long within the inner sanctuary. When at last the old man came out, his lips were moving silently, and his hands made gestures in the air as if he had been taken with a sudden illness. As they stared at him, astonished, they became aware that some strange and wonderful thing had happened to him. All he could do was beckon to them dumbly and make signs that he had lost his speech, yet on his face there was a radiance that they had never seen before. It came to them, then, that he must have seen a vision in the temple, and they were filled with awe. They waited for some time to see what else might happen or what he might say when he regained his voice, but there was no sign. The old man remained speechless for all the time they waited, until at last they went away and forgot what they had seen.

When Zacharias was finished with his days of duty in the temple, he departed to his own house in the rolling hills of Judea. He still could not speak nor did he speak for several months thereafter. But soon after he came home his wife, Elisabeth, told him that they were, at last, to have a child.

TO ST. JOHN THE BAPTIST

Thou last of prophets,
Born like Samuel
Didst from a womb
Past hope of issue come.
His mother silent spake;
Thy father dumb,
Recovering speech,
God's wonder did foretell.
And thou unborn
Within thy mother's womb,
He did anoint the king,
Whom God did take
From charge of sheep
To rule His chosen land.
But that high King who
Heaven and earth did make,
Received a holier liquor
From thy hand,
When God His flock
In human shape did feed,
As Israel's king kept his
In shepherd's weed.

HENRY CONSTABLE

This scale model of the Temple in Jerusalem shows the massive walls and porticos which set the Temple apart from the surrounding city of Jerusalem. Photo by Thomas R. Fletcher.

On Jordan's Bank

On Jordan's bank
    the Baptist's cry
Announces that
    the Lord is nigh:
Awake and hearken,
    for he brings
Glad tidings
    of the King of kings.

Then cleansed be
    every heart from sin;
Make straight the way
    of God within,
And let each heart
    prepare a home
Where such a mighty
    guest may come.

For You are our salvation,
    Lord,
Our refuge
    and our great reward;
Without Your grace
    we waste away
Like flowers that wither
    and decay.

All praise the Son eternally,
Whose advent
    sets His people free,
Whom with the Father
    we adore
And Spirit blest for evermore.

CHARLES COFFIN

The Jordan River connects the Sea of Galilee with the Dead Sea and provides irrigation to the Jordan River Valley. John baptized Jesus in the Jordan River, and the Holy Spirit descended upon Him as a dove. Photo of the Jordan River in northern Galilee by Alan and Sandy Carey.

And You Will Name Him John

ANTHONY BURGESS

he priest said, "John? There is none of your family or of the family of his father so called. This is irregular."

Elisabeth said, "In the temple when my husband was vouchsafed the vision and the prophecy, this name was given to him. And this name is John."

"We must," the priest said, "have the word from his father's mouth, and in his father's mouth there is no word."

But Zacharias made gestures showing that he wished a tablet and a stylus to be brought. Almost at once, in the act of beginning to write, Zacharias found that his tongue was, after nine months silence, loosed. Zacharias said, firmly and quietly, "His name is John."

There was general astonishment, and some went down on their knees. Zacharias, as if to make up for the long enforced dumbness, became voluble and prophetic. His son howled, and the father shouted him down.

He said, "Blessed be the Lord, the God of Israel. For He has visited us and wrought redemption for His people. He has raised for us a horn of salvation in the house of His servant David." John was so loud that his mother rocked and hushed him, but he only bellowed the louder. "And what He spoke through the mouths of the holy prophets shall be fulfilled: salvation from our enemies, and from the hand of all that hate us, mercy to His people, who shall serve Him without fear, in holiness and righteousness before Him all our days.

"And you, my child, whose voice is already great and shall be greater still in the Lord's service, you shall be called the Prophet of the Most High, for you shall go before the face of the Lord to make ready His path, to give knowledge of salvation to His people, in the remission of their sins because of the tender mercy of our God."

THE BETROTHAL

FATHER PRAT

he little village of Nazareth, where heaven was mysteriously wedded to earth in the person of Jesus, was at the time of our story only an unknown, straggling village.

Despite her youth, Mary was betrothed to a kinsman named Joseph, sprung like herself from the tribe of Judah and the house of David. With the Hebrews, betrothal was not a simple promise of marriage as it is with us. It had the effect of a marriage, with its mutual rights and duties and all its juridical consequences. "Betrothal," writes Philo, a contemporary of Jesus, "has the same force as marriage."

In Deuteronomy, as in the Gospels, the betrothed girl is called the wife of her fiance, since that is what she actually was. If she is unfaithful, she is punished as an adulteress. If her fiance dies, she is considered a widow and benefits by the Law of Levirate, which obliges the brother of her deceased and childless husband to marry her. She can be repudiated only with the formalities required in the case of a legitimate wife. One difference, however, was that cohabitation was generally postponed, sometimes for as long as a year or even longer. This was done to give the husband an opportunity to fulfill the onerous clauses in the contract or to allow the virgin, who was ordinarily betrothed as a young girl, to come of age in her father's house. It was then that the wedding festivities took place, varying with the circumstances of those concerned, but always as solemn as the position and means of the bride and groom permitted.

Betrothals were sometimes sealed in writing but more often concluded by word of mouth. In the presence of two witnesses, the man offered his betrothed a small gift and said to her, "By this token you are my betrothed." She answered by accepting the gift. The pact was usually ratified by a private meal at the home of the girl's father.

MARY

This is the blessed Mary,
    pre-elect
God's virgin.
Gone is a great while,
    and she
Dwelt young in Nazareth
    of Galilee.
Unto God's will she brought
    devout respect,
Profound simplicity
    of intellect,
And supreme patience.
    From her mother's knee
Faithful and hopeful,
    wise in charity,
Strong in grave peace,
    in pity circumspect.
So held she through
    her girlhood, as it were
An angel-watered lily,
    that near God
Grows and is quiet.
    Till, one day at home
She woke in her white bed,
    and had no fear
At all—yet wept
    till sunshine and felt awed
Because the fullness
    of the time was come.

DANTE GABRIEL ROSSETTI

In ancient Israel betrothals were a legal matter, not just a simple engagement. Marriages were arranged between families; often the bride-to-be was as young as twelve years old. Giuseppe Passeri's THE MARRIAGE OF THE VIRGIN *(Christie's Images/SuperStock) may depict the Rabbi's blessing during a betrothal ceremony.*

THE ANGEL GABRIEL APPEARS TO MARY

nd in the sixth month the angel Gabriel was sent from God unto a city of Galilee, named Nazareth, to a virgin espoused to a man whose name was Joseph, of the house of David; and the virgin's name was Mary.

And the angel came in unto her, and said, Hail, thou that art highly favoured, the Lord is with thee: blessed art thou among women.

And when she saw him, she was troubled at his saying, and cast in her mind what manner of salutation this should be.

And the angel said unto her, Fear not, Mary: for thou hast found favour with God. And, behold, thou shalt conceive in thy womb, and bring forth a Son, and shalt call his name JESUS. He shall be great, and shall be called the Son of the Highest, and the Lord God shall give unto Him the throne of His father David: And He shall reign over the house of Jacob for ever; and of His kingdom there shall be no end.

Then said Mary unto the angel, How shall this be, seeing I know not a man?

And the angel answered and said unto her, The Holy Ghost shall come upon thee, and the power of the Highest shall overshadow thee: therefore also that holy thing which shall be born of thee shall be called the Son of God. And, behold, thy cousin Elisabeth, she hath also conceived a son in her old age: and this is the sixth month with her, who was called barren. For with God nothing shall be impossible.

And Mary said, Behold the handmaid of the Lord; be it unto me according to thy word. And the angel departed from her (*Luke 1:26–38*).

Lorenzo di Credi's THE ANNUNCIATION *(Galleria Degli Uffizi/SuperStock) illustrates the angel Gabriel's tender announcement to Mary. His good news must have startled the young woman.*

BLESSED AMONG WOMEN

FULTON OURSLER

ary had undergone a change. It was an experience shattering to the very roots of her being. For hours after it happened she was unable to speak; she could scarcely even breathe. It was so inexplicable, so dazing, so frightening that for the time she could not force herself to tell even Joseph.

How could she ask him to believe that she had actually known such a wonder?

Yet she had known it. Without one instant's preparation she had walked into it, immediately after that tender good night at the gate. The hens and rooster were perched and asleep, the dog was out barking behind the garden, and the sheep and goats were dozing.

Feeling a little chill, for the night was damp, Mary had crossed the lower floor inside the house and mounted to the inner terrace. As she went up the steps to the platform, she realized that she was not alone. A tall figure was standing near the farther wall.

A stranger. An odd and altogether different stranger! He seemed to stand in light where there was no lamp, and a kind of silvery mist enveloped him as if the light were his cap and gown. Mary opened her mouth to speak, to demand who he was and what he wanted there, but he anticipated her with an unexpected greeting.

"Hail, Mary!"

The voice was kind and fathomlessly deep, such a voice as Mary had never heard before, bass and yet tender. "Full of grace!" the voice continued.

Hail, Mary, full of grace! She felt embarrassed and even more frightened.

"The Lord is with you. Blessed are you among women."

She folded her hands and she knew then how she was

TRADITIONAL ENGLISH CAROL

He came all so still
Where His mother was,
As dew in April
That falleth on the grass.

He came all so still
To His mother's bower,
As dew in April
That falleth on the flower.

He came all so still
Where His mother lay,
As dew in April
That falleth on the spray.

Mother and maiden
Was never none but she,
Well may such a lady
Jesus' mother be.

AUTHOR UNKNOWN

THERE IS NO ROSE

There is no rose
   of such virtue
As is the rose
   that bare Jesu;
Alleluia.

For in this rose
   containëd was
Heaven and earth
   in little space;
Res miranda.

By that rose we may
   well see
That He is God
   in persons three,
Pari forma.

The angels sang
   the shepherds too:
Gloria in excelsis deo:
Gaudeamus.

Leave we all
   this worldly mirth,
And follow we
   this joyful birth;
Transeamus.

           AUTHOR UNKNOWN

trembling in every muscle. The stranger saw.

"Fear not, Mary."

She bowed her head. She must not be afraid. She knew she could trust this deep and tender voice. But she could not still her quaking. She closed her eyes and listened to the astounding words this stranger was speaking to her. She had found grace with God. She would conceive in her womb and bring forth a son.

"And you shall call His name Jesus."

"Jesus! He will be my son. Jesus! Jesus, son of Mary! I shall bring Him forth and hold Him in my arms and sometimes I shall give Him to Joseph to hold too!" Her mind was a place of wild, birdlike thoughts; yet she must listen to all that the stranger continued to tell her: her son, Jesus, was to have the throne of David, his father—

"And of all his kingdom there shall be no end."

Then came her instant need for reality. Who this stranger was she did not know; yet the maiden who heard his words felt bound to question him. "How shall this be done?" she asked in a whisper. "Seeing I know not a man?"

But there came no frown on the austere and shadowy face of the stranger. Instead, in the starry blaze of his eyes she read only compassion. He took a step nearer, and she saw the folded wings and knew him for what he was.

His voice was lower and deeper still, "The Holy Ghost shall come upon you. The power of the Most High shall overshadow you and the child which shall be born of you shall be called the Son of God."

Mary felt stifled, suffocated as she heard these incredible words. She was to be the mother of a son who would be called the Son of God?

How could one little Nazareth girl take all that in? She looked up at him plaintively, her eyes half-closed, her words coming so softly that she could barely hear herself speak. "Behold the handmaid of the Lord. Be it done unto me according to your word."

The angel vanished, and Mary, swaying and murmuring, sank to her knees, closed her eyes, and wept and prayed.

THE ANGEL GABRIEL

The angel Gabriel
    from heaven came,
His wings as drifted snow,
    His eyes as flame;
"All hail," said he,
    "Thou lowly maiden Mary,
Most highly favoured lady, gloria!

"For known a blessèd mother
    thou shalt be,
All generations laud
    and honor thee,
Thy Son shall be Emmanuel,
    by seers foretold."
Most highly favoured lady, gloria!

Then gentle Mary meekly
    bowed her head,
"To me be as it pleaseth God,"
    she said.
"My soul shall laud
    and magnify His Holy Name."
Most highly favoured lady, gloria!

Of her, Emmanuel,
    the Christ, was born
In Bethlehem
    all on a Christmas morn.
And Christian folk
    throughout the world will ever say:
Most highly favoured lady, gloria!

SABINE BARING-GOULD

In Giorgio Vasari's THE ANNUNCIATION
(Musee du Louvre/SuperStock) the angel
Gabriel holds a lily, a flower which symbolizes
innocence and purity. Vasari depicts the Holy
Ghost who descended upon Mary as a dove.

THE ANNUNCIATION

And was it true, the stranger standing so,
And saying things that lifted her in two?
Her eyes filled slowly with the morning glow.
Her drowsy ear drank in a first sweet dubious bird.

Her cheek against the pillow woke and stirred
To gales enriched by passage over dew,
And friendly fields and slopes of Galilee
Arose in tremulous intermixture with her dreams,
Till she remembered suddenly . . .

Although the morning beams
Came spilling in the gradual rubric known to every day,
And hills stood black and ruinous as in eclipse
Against the softly spreading ray,
Not touched by any strange apocalypse
Though nothing was disturbed from where she lay and saw,
Now she remembered with a quick and panting awe
That someone came, and took in hand her heart,
And broke it irresistibly apart
With what he said, and how in tall suspense
He lingered while the white celestial inference,
Pushing her fears apart, went softly home.

Then she had faltered her reply
And felt the sudden burden of eternal years,
And shamed by the angelic stranger standing by,
Had bowed her head to hide her human tears.

Never again would she awake
And find herself the buoyant Galilean lass,
But into her dissolving dreams would break
A hovering consciousness too terrible to pass:
A new awareness in her body when she stirred,
A sense of Light within her virgin gloom.
She was the mother of the wandering Word,
Little and terrifying in her laboring womb.

And nothing would again be casual and small,
But everything with light invested, overspilled
With terror and divinity, the dawn, the first bird's call,
The silhouetted pitcher waiting to be filled.

JOHN DUFFY

JESUS' WORLD

A carpenter's workshop usually occupied the bottom floor of his home. The family lived either above or behind the shop.

Carpenters used few tools—an adze, a saw, a mallet and chisels, a hammer, a shaver, and perhaps sandstone, to smooth the wood.

During Jesus' time, children were important in maintaining a strong family. Children helped their parents with the family work, continued the family line, kept the family property intact, and cared for aging relatives.

Jesus probably helped Joseph in his carpenter's shop. It was customary for boys to begin training in their father's profession while they were young. Later, when their fathers became too old to work, the sons would take over the family business.

The hilltop town of Nazareth is located near the city of Sepphoris and on the trade route between Ptolemais and Tiberias. Photo of Nazareth from Gabriel's Bell Tower by Thomas R. Fletcher.

The formal betrothal ritual took place as long as twelve months before the wedding and was performed in the presence of witnesses. During the ceremony, the father of the groom paid a sum of money to the bride's father and gave an assurance that the families would be united.

Guests who were invited to a wedding were called "children of the bride chamber." They participated in the procession and held palm and myrtle branches as a canopy over the couple's heads.

On the night of a marriage, young women went forth with lamps or torches to meet the bridegroom and escort him to the bride's house.

Betrothals could only be broken by a formal divorce.

When the angel Gabriel appeared to Zacharias, he was performing the honor of burning incense in the holy of holies in the Temple in Jerusalem. Photo by Richard T. Nowitz.

Following the tradition of the time, Mary lived with her parents during her betrothal. Photo of what is traditionally considered to be the excavated remains of Mary's house by Kay Shaw.

Like most sons of carpenters, Jesus probably served as Joseph's apprentice, sitting beside him and crafting plows, yokes, and other farm equipment or various household items.

THE ANGEL APPEARS TO JOSEPH

ow the birth of Jesus Christ was on this wise: When as his mother Mary was espoused to Joseph, before they came together, she was found with child of the Holy Ghost.

Then Joseph her husband, being a just man, and not willing to make her a publick example, was minded to put her away privily.

But while he thought on these things, behold, the angel of the Lord appeared unto him in a dream, saying, Joseph, thou son of David, fear not to take unto thee Mary thy wife: for that which is conceived in her is of the Holy Ghost. And she shall bring forth a Son, and thou shalt call His name JESUS: for He shall save his people from their sins.

Now all this was done, that it might be fulfilled which was spoken of the Lord by the prophet saying, Behold a virgin shall be with child and shall bring forth a son, and they shall call his name Emmanuel, which being interpreted is, God with us.

Then Joseph being raised from sleep did as the angel of the Lord had bidden him, and took unto him his wife, and knew her not till she had brought forth her firstborn son: and he called His name JESUS (*Matthew 1:18–25*).

In the Bible, God often uses dreams as a means to communicate with His people. Before and after Christ's birth, the angel of the Lord appeared to Joseph in a dream. Painted on the walls of the Arena Chapel in Padua, Italy, Giotto di Bondone's JOSEPH'S DREAM *(Arena Chapel/SuperStock) captures the wonder of this dream announcement.*

A Prophecy Fulfilled

Sholem Asch

oseph threw himself upon his couch and began pondering what to do next. He felt no resentment against Miriam, for he knew in his heart that he could not charge her with faithlessness. He was certain there was something she had wished to tell him but had left unsaid. Her eyes had spoken to him with an articulateness of their own, so that only the grossness of his understanding had prevented him from grasping their meaning. The hope of the world was in her womb, she had said. He had not understood and did not now, but the deathless joy of her eyes had confirmed her words, placed them beyond the reach of questioning and prying doubt. With such radiance, no sin could be mingled; it did not call for pity, only for a sharing of joy.

He had taken upon himself all there was of responsibility, had publicly confessed himself the author of whatever shame had been committed. Miriam was safe from the law, nothing could touch her now. And as for him, the only thing remaining was to retire from her sight. Of course, he could not go without the curses of the town at his back. They would say that he had married a poor girl only to forsake her and to leave a sullied name behind. But there was no help for it. Later, from a distance, he would be able to send a bill of divorcement as prescribed by the Law of Israel. He would willingly pay any price to spare Miriam the shame and distress of his presence, that she might stand guiltless before her family and the people of Nazareth.

It would not take him long to leave the town. There were some hours yet before dawn. Until then he would rest, for his eyes were heavy and the harrowing of the day had exhausted his body. His lids fell shut. And Joseph saw his couch stir, rocking at first, then sway and lift itself and soar

The Birth of Christ

The time draws near
    the birth of Christ;
The moon is hid;
    the night is still;
The Christmas bells
    from hill to hill
Answer each other
    in the mist.

Four voices
    of four hamlets round,
From far and near,
    on mead and moor,
Swell out and fail,
    as if a door
Were shut between me
    and the sound.

Each voice four changes
    on the wind,
That now dilate
    and now decrease,
Peace and good-will,
    good will and peace,
Peace and good-will
    to all mankind.

Rise, happy morn!
    rise, holy morn!
Draw forth the cheerful day
    from night;
O Father! touch the east,
    and light
The light that shone
    when hope was born!

Alfred, Lord Tennyson

Joseph had descended from the house of David in Bethlehem but lived in Nazareth, fifteen miles southwest of the Sea of Galilee. The Sea of Galilee is a freshwater lake twelve-and-a-half-miles long and seven miles wide at its widest point. Photo of mustard plants blooming by the Sea of Galilee by Thomas R. Fletcher.

with him beyond the reach of clouds. He felt himself carried up into measureless heights and into a sea of light. It was too luminous for human eyes, and Joseph saw nothing but the blinding brightness of it, nothing but a face, fulgent and infinite, a sun of suns. The face bent over him, and Joseph felt the timid pressure of an all-pervading softness and saw the shade of two limitless wings falling about his couch. He thought he lay like Jacob in the arms of a seraph and heard a voice speaking to him: "Joseph, fear not to take your bride Miriam to wife, for that which is conceived in her is of the Holy Ghost. She will bear a son and you shall call his name Yeshua, for He will save His people from their sins."

Joseph awoke with his heart beating wildly. Sweat trickled from his forehead, and his limbs shook uncontrollably. He was afraid of his vision, and yet he felt a gush of happiness within his body. The bitter recollection of the previous day was gone. The world around was bright and shadowless, and Joseph's heart leaped for joy.

JOSEPH'S ACCEPTANCE

ALICE DARTON

oseph noticed the intangible change that had come over Mary's character, the radiance that shone from her shyly raised eyes, the inward joy she seemed trying to conceal. Joseph noticed something else too. The maiden whose childlike modesty, whose angelic virtues had won his tenderest affections, was to become a mother.

How could he reconcile this with all that he had believed of Mary, with what he knew of her life, of her upbringing, her character? His being was shaken to its foundations, for if Mary were capable of what the malicious would be quick to suspect, how could he ever have faith in human nature again?

He had loved her dearly; he had desired to cherish her, and even now he could not bear to think of her as a target for the world's revilement and criticism. His sense of justice demanded that he shut her out from his heart, but he could not endure to divorce her publicly, as was his right.

He considered these matters sadly, wavering in favor of the maiden whom by human standards he was justified in casting aside, inclining to sacrifice himself rather than let her be exposed to contempt.

Not until he had made up his mind to the kind and generous course did God interfere. Then after he had fallen asleep, tired with the emotional ordeal, the angel of the Lord appeared to him in his sleep, saying, "Joseph, son of David, fear not to take unto thee Mary thy wife, for that which is conceived in her is of the Holy Ghost. And she shall bring forth a son; and thou shalt call his name Jesus. For he shall save his people from their sins."

How gently, almost reverently, the angel addressed this noble man. Joseph awoke with a paean of joy in his soul. His world had righted itself. Mary was restored in his heart and seated there more securely than before. She had been

THE CARPENTER'S SON

"Son, fit the grooves
And join them well;
These yokes must be both
Strong and light.
The yokes of Joseph
Shall be safe,
Nor oxen's weary
Shoulders chafe—
Have patience, Son,
And build aright."

The carpenter of Nazareth
Thus kindly spake
Unto his Son,
Nor dreamed those busy
Hands would be
Pierced by the nails
Of Calvary
Before their mission
Should be done.

"My yoke is easy,"
Spake the Man
Who trod the hills
Of Galilee.
"The yoke I give is strong
And safe;
My yoke will never gall
Nor chafe
A weary soul; come—
Follow Me!"

KATHRYN BLACKBURN PECK

Joseph was a carpenter in Nazareth and probably instructed his son in the trade. When Jesus began His ministry, the people in Nazareth were shocked. "Is not this the carpenter's son?" they asked. Despite Jesus' training at the synagogue, He would have only been seen as a carpenter in the city of His youth. J. R. Herbert's YOUTH OF OUR LORD (Guildhall Art Gallery/Super-Stock) illustrates the plain surroundings of Joseph's shop, the place where Jesus "grew and waxed strong in spirit."

chosen by the Holy Ghost. And her child, Jesus—his heart leaped out to the babe. The Promised One was coming; God was showing Israel mercy once again; the great day was dawning for which His people and His house had been longing through centuries of sorrow and dismay.

Joseph sought Mary at once. Well did he now understand that irradiation of her being with joy; he felt it flooding his own heart. Mary recognized it in him before a single word was spoken. Their eyes, meeting, flashed the message of a happy comprehension. God had again provided a confidant for Mary and another home in which she should be safe.

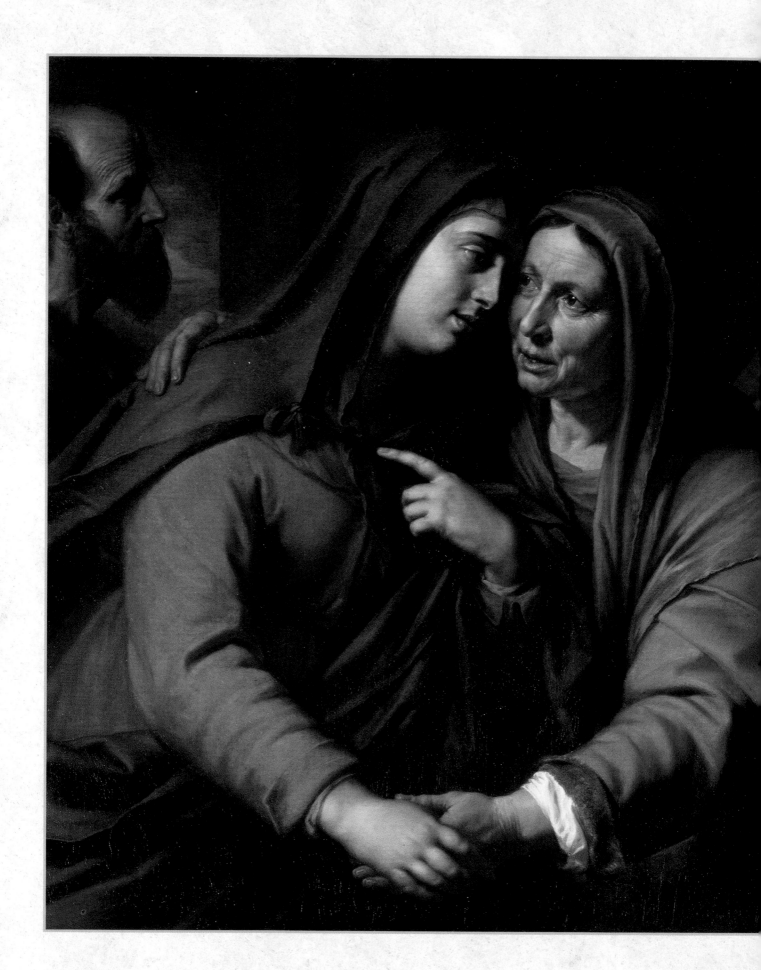

THE VISITATION

nd Mary arose in those days, and went into the hill country with haste, into a city of Judah; And entered into the house of Zacharias, and saluted Elisabeth.

And it came to pass, that, when Elisabeth heard the salutation of Mary, the babe leaped in her womb, and Elisabeth was filled with the Holy Ghost; And she spake out with a loud voice and said, Blessed art thou among women, and blessed is the fruit of thy womb.

And whence is this to me, that the mother of my Lord should come to me? For, lo, as soon as the voice of thy salutation sounded in mine ears, the babe leaped in my womb for joy. And blessed is she that believed: for there shall be a performance of those things which were told her from the Lord.

And Mary said, My soul doth magnify the Lord, And my spirit hath rejoiced in God my Saviour. For He hath regarded the low estate of his handmaiden: for, behold, from henceforth all generations shall call me blessed.

For he that is mighty hath done to me great things; and holy is his name. And his mercy is on them that fear Him from generation to generation.

He hath showed strength with his arm; he hath scattered the proud in the imagination of their hearts. He hath put down the mighty from their seats, and exalted them of low degree. He hath filled the hungry with good things; and the rich he hath sent empty away. He hath helped his servant Israel, in remembrance of his mercy; As he spake to our fathers, to Abraham, and to his seed for ever (*Luke 1:39–55*).

When Mary arrived at the home of Elisabeth and Zacharias, Elisabeth was immediately filled with the Holy Spirit and called Mary the "mother of my Lord." Philippe de Champaigne's THE VISITATION (Christie's Images/SuperStock) captures the tender greeting and the excitement between these two godly women.

Mary and Elisabeth

Martin Luther

hen Mary heard that her cousin Elisabeth was with child, she set out to help her. Mary was of royal lineage and was to be the true, natural mother of Jesus. Yet she set out on foot on a journey of two or three days to do maid service for Elisabeth. Shame on us for all our pride! No peasant and no townsman of good family among us would stoop so far. If one of us is descended from a noble or a prince, there is no end of bragging. Yet, though she was carrying the Son of God, she was willing to be a maid.

"When Elisabeth heard the salutation of Mary, the babe leaped in her womb." John knew before his mother that Mary was carrying the Saviour. When he leaped in the womb, his mother perceived what she had not discerned by the sight of the eyes, for Mary's condition was not yet evident.

Elisabeth was then so overcome that she did not thank Mary, nor did she greet her with the familiarity of a kinswoman but said instead: "Blessed art thou among women, and blessed is the fruit of thy womb. And whence is this to me, that the mother of my Lord should come to me?" Elisabeth forgot that Mary was of royal blood and called her only mother and the mother of the Lord. One humility confronted another. Mary humbled herself, and Elisabeth considered herself unworthy to have her come, though she was very pleased. Then she explained why she had forgotten to welcome her and thanked her because at her word the babe leaped in her womb. And then she added, "Blessed is she that hath believed."

In Mary and Elisabeth we see how mighty a thing is genuine faith, for it changes a person in soul and body. Elisabeth had become another woman full of inexpressible joy. Her body and tongue were so joyous that she became a prophetess.

The Visitation

To Elisabeth she came,
over the hills,
bearing the Lord
flowering in her womb—
sacrament of her flesh,
bud richly taut—
the warmth of her
containing His infinity,
the sun His fire.

The dark earth of her body
seemed to encompass all things.
The terraced fields of Judah
pregnant with seed
called out to her
as she passed,
praising the Child
she was yet to bear,
invoking His blessing
on their expectancy.

These must call out,
full in their fullness,
barren beside hers,
then how should a child
six months conceived
adore with stillness
in his mother's womb?

Calvin Le Compte

Mary left "with haste" to see her cousin, Elisabeth, who was six months pregnant. Her trip from Nazareth to the Judean hill-country outside Jerusalem would have taken her through olive groves dotted with poppies and other wildflowers. Photo of olive trees in Israel's hill-country by Saul Mayer/New England Stock.

THE JOURNEY TO BETHLEHEM

A thrill of hope, the weary
world rejoices, for yonder
breaks a new and glorious morn.

JOSEPH AND MARY JOURNEY TO BETHLEHEM

And it came to pass in those days, that there went out a decree from Caesar Augustus that all the world should be taxed. (And this taxing was first made when Cyrenius was governor of Syria.)

And all went to be taxed, every one into his own city.

And Joseph also went up from Galilee, out of the city of Nazareth, into Judaea, unto the city of David, which is called Bethlehem; (because he was of the house of lineage of David:) to be taxed with Mary his espoused wife, being great with child (*Luke 2:1–5*).

Anton Becker's PASSAGE TO BETHLEHEM *(SuperStock) illustrates the great care Joseph must have taken with his beloved wife and the Child she carried as they journeyed ninety miles over rugged terrain.*

BETHLEHEM

FULTON J. SHEEN

aesar Augustus, the master bookkeeper of the world, sat in his palace by the Tiber. Before him was stretched a map labeled *Orbis Terrarum, Imperium Romanum*. He was about to issue an order for a census of the world, for all the nations of the civilized world were subject to Rome. There was only one capital in the world: Rome; only one official language: Latin; only one ruler: Caesar. To every outpost, to every satrap and governor, the order went out: every Roman subject must be enrolled in his own city. On the fringe of the Empire, in the little village of Nazareth, soldiers tacked upon walls the order for all the citizens to register in the towns of their family origins.

Joseph, the builder, an obscure descendant of the great King David, was obliged by that very fact to register in Bethlehem, the city of David. In accordance with the edict, Mary and Joseph set out from the village of Nazareth for the village of Bethlehem which lies about five miles on the other side of Jerusalem. Five hundred years earlier the prophet Micah had prophesied concerning that little village;

> *And thou, Bethlehem, in the land of Judah, art not the least among the princes of Judah: for out of thee shall come a Governor, that shall rule my people Israel (Matthew 2:6).*

Joseph was full of expectancy as he entered the city of his family and was quite convinced that he would have no difficulty in finding lodgings for Mary, particularly on account of her condition. Joseph went from house to house only to find each one crowded. He searched in vain for a place where He, to whom heaven and earth belonged, might be born. Could it be that the Creator would find a home in creation? Up a steep hill Joseph climbed to a faint light which swung on a rope across a doorway. This would be the village inn. There, above all other places, he would surely find shelter. There was room in the inn for the soldiers of Rome who had brutally subjugated the Jewish peo-

THE BIRDS OF BETHLEHEM

I heard the bells
   of Bethlehem ring;
Their voice was sweeter
   than the priest's;
I heard the birds
   of Bethlehem sing
Unbidden in the
   churchly feasts.

They clung and sung
   on the swinging chain
High in the dim and
   incensed air;
The priests, with
   repetitions vain,
Chanted a never-ending prayer.

So bell and bird
   and priest I heard,
But voice of bird was most
   to me;
It had no ritual, no word,
And yet it sounded true
   and free.

I thought Child Jesus,
   were He there,
Would like the singing birds
   the best,
And clutch His little
   hands in air
And smile upon His
   mother's breast.

RICHARD WATSON GILDER

LONG, LONG AGO

Winds through the olive trees
Softly did blow,
Round little Bethlehem
Long, long ago.

Sheep on the hillside lay
Whiter than snow;
Shepherds were watching them,
Long, long ago.

Then from the happy sky,
Angels bent low,
Singing their songs of joy,
Long, long ago.

For in a manger bed,
Cradled we know,
Christ came to Bethlehem
Long, long ago.

AUTHOR UNKNOWN

ple; there was room for the daughters of the rich merchants of the East; there was room for those clothed in soft garments, who lived in houses of the king; in fact, there was room for anyone who had a coin to give the innkeeper; but there was no room for Him who came to be the inn of every homeless heart in the world. When finally the scrolls of history are completed down to the last words in time, the saddest line of all will be: "There was no room in the inn."

In the filthiest place in the world, a stable, Purity was born. He, who was later to be slaughtered by men acting as beasts, was born among beasts. He, who would call Himself the "living Bread descended from Heaven," was laid in a manger, literally, a place to eat. Centuries before, the Jews had worshiped the golden calf, and the Greeks, the ass. Men bowed down before them as before God. The ox and the ass now were present to make their innocent reparation, bowing down before their God.

There was no room in the inn, but there was room in the stable. The inn is the gathering place of public opinion, the local point of the world's moods, the rendezvous of the worldly, the rallying place of the popular and the successful. But the stable is a place for the outcasts, the ignored, the forgotten. The world might have expected the Son of God to be born—if He was to be born at all—in an inn. A stable would be the last place in the world where one would have looked for Him. Divinity is always where one least expects to find it.

No worldly mind would ever have suspected that He who could make the sun warm the earth would one day have need of an ox and an ass to warm Him with their breath; that He, who clothed the fields with grass, would Himself be naked; that He, from whose hands came planets and worlds, would one day have tiny arms that were not long enough to touch the huge heads of the cattle; that His feet which would trod the everlasting hills would one day be too weak to walk; that the Eternal Word would be dumb; that Omnipotence would be wrapped in swaddling clothes; that Salvation would lie in a manger; that God coming to this earth would ever be so helpless.

How Far to Bethlehem?

"How far is it to Bethlehem Town?"
Just over Jerusalem hills and down,
Past lovely Rachel's white-domed tomb—
Sweet shrine of motherhood's young doom.

"It isn't far to Bethlehem Town—
Just over the dusty roads and down,
Past Wise Men's well, still offering
Cool draughts from welcome wayside spring;
Past shepherds with their flutes of reed
That charm the woolly sheep they lead;
Past boys with kites on hilltops flying,
And soon you're there where Bethlehem's lying.
Sunned white and sweet on olived slopes,
Gold-lighted still with Judah's hopes.

"And so we find the Shepherd's field
And plain that gave rich Boaz yield,
And look where Herod's villa stood.
We thrill that earthly parenthood
Could foster Christ who was all-good
And thrill that Bethlehem Town to-day
Looks down on Christmas homes that pray.

"It isn't far to Bethlehem Town!
It's anywhere that Christ comes down
And finds in people's friendly face
A welcome and abiding place.
The road to Bethlehem runs right through
The homes of folks like me and you."

Madeleine Sweeny Miller

The journey to Bethlehem could have taken Joseph and Mary almost five days. The Roman Empire built a vast network of roads to move their armies more easily; it is possible that Joseph and Mary took one of these better roads. David Roberts's The Descent to the Valley of Jordan *(Newberry Library/SuperStock) shows the rough terrain surrounding one of these roads.*

BOUND FOR BETHLEHEM

HENRY DANIEL-ROPS

hat do we know of this couple who set out on the road to obey the order of Caesar? They were united by the sacred tie of marriage and, moreover, by affection, for it was not essential that the young wife in her condition should have accompanied her husband since only males were required to present themselves for registration. They were poor people of the working class, richer in courage than in money.

Though they were both so humble, it need not surprise us that they belonged to Israel's royal family. Not all of the innumerable descendants of David and Solomon were rich or in high places. It would seem that both Joseph and Mary were of the line of David. In the case of Joseph it is expressly stated in the gospels, by Matthew at the beginning of his book and by Luke when he comes to the account of the public ministry of Jesus; there it was important, because it was known that the Messiah would be born of the race of the great king. And so Joseph and Mary set out for Bethlehem, the town which the sacred writings had designated as the birthplace of the Messiah. For it was of Bethlehem that the prophet Micah had said, "But thou, Beth-lehem Ephratah, though thou be little among the thousands of Judah, yet out of thee shall he come forth unto me that is to be ruler in Israel."

Joseph and Mary would remember this prophecy, for they knew that the child which Mary bore was the pledge of a miracle. So great would be the hope in their hearts that it might well seem that it was for this that Caesar all unknowing had signed his decree and mobilized his army of functionaries, for the ways of God are obscure to men and the mightiest are but instruments in His hands.

WE JOURNEY THERE

Come, let us cross
   the snows on Christmas Eve
And, like the shepherds,
   seek the lowly shed
Wherein the cattle
   and the sheep perceive
A sleeping Child,
   their manger for His bed.

Come, let us go
   to ancient Bethlehem
This starry night
   when miracles occur,
When kings
   from far beyond Jerusalem
Bring gifts of gold
   and frankincense and myrrh.

O never doubt
   that we find the way
Across the world
   to that Judaean town,
And never doubt
   that we shall kneel to pray
While angel-song
   comes slowly drifting down.

Each Christmas Eve,
   with neither maps nor charts,
We journey there—
   directed by our hearts.

BERYL STEWART

Jesus' ancestor David worked as a shepherd in the hills surrounding Bethlehem. In these fields he tended his flock and played his lyre to pass the lonely hours. Photo of Shepherd's Fields outside Bethlehem by Richard T. Nowitz.

THE THREE STRANGERS

RICHARD P. OLSON

he night was dark and overcast, damp and chilly. A noisy wind blew eerily around houses and down narrow roads. This darkness was all the deeper in the gloomy, winding streets of Bethlehem. Two men hurried down the street toward each other, unaware of the other's presence. They pulled their garments up over their heads for warmth as they made their way down the alley.

Suddenly they collided. Both thought they had been attacked and grabbed for their weapons. One drew a Roman sword from the sheath at his side, the other a short dagger from the cord that held his inner garment. They stood, tensed, staring into the darkness. Without speaking, they nodded to each other and turned to go. Shortly, both arrived at the same small inn.

The larger man was a Roman centurion. His name was Artemus. The thinner, shorter, wiry man was an Arab shepherd. His name was Ishmael.

Their eyes turned to the room they had entered. Though the rest of Bethlehem had seemed deserted, this place was not. It was filled with people. From the far end of the room, they saw an older man sitting at a small table by himself. Squinting, he looked toward them and vaguely waved his hand, beckoning Artemus and Ishmael. Each took the invitation to be for himself, and each made his way by separate routes. At about the same time, both arrived at the table of the older man. He was stocky with a tinge of gray in both his hair and beard. This man, the innkeeper, was a Jew by the name of Mordecai.

Without speaking to one another, each ordered his drink and sipped in silence. Most of the time they looked down into their cups, but occasionally their eyes met

BETHLEHEM TOWN

As I was going
To Bethlehem town
Upon the earth
I cast me down
All underneath a tree,
That whispered
In this wise to me:
"Oh! I shall stand
On Calvary
And bear what burden
Saveth thee!"
As up I fared
To Bethlehem town.

Again I walk
In Bethlehem town
And think on Him
That wears the crown.
I may not kiss His feet again,
Nor worship Him
As I did then;
My King hath died
Upon the tree
And hath outpoured
On Calvary
What Blood redeemeth
You and me!

EUGENE FIELD

Many of Bethlehem's streets are narrow because of the city's hillside location. This alleyway, where an old woman sits on the steps beside the Church of the Nativity, is typical of many of the narrow passageways that dot this city. Photo of Bethlehem alleyway by Richard T. Nowitz.

uneasily, and the silence seemed strained. Three men who would never meet socially were crowded at a little table. They were uncomfortable but did not know what to do.

Ishmael was an outgoing man who did not like silence. It was he who first spoke. Turning to Artemus he asked, "How's the occupation going?"

"You know, all of us dread assignment to Judea. Other places where I've been don't like to be ruled by Rome either. But here, it's as if the people are never conquered. There is always something stirring. I hope I'm not here when the revolution comes. It will be a battle to the end. For we are just here on assignment, but these people fight in the name of their God for everything they believe in and stand for."

Mordecai and Ishmael looked at each other, surprised to hear such sentiments from a respected Roman centurion. They relaxed a bit. Mordecai asked, "Is the census finished?"

Artemus responded, "I will give Quirinius credit for a stroke of genius for having each of them go to the city of their ancestors. That seemed to touch some feeling of national pride so that the resistance wasn't as bad as feared. It was strange, at the census. Let me tell you about the strangest one of all!"

Mordecai and Ishmael leaned close. Artemus exclaimed, "One man laughed! Yes, that's true. When he came and I asked, 'How many people do you register?' 'Two that you can count', he said, and burst out laughing. Then I saw his wife standing, waiting for him. She was very, very pregnant. I smiled as if I understood. I could see that a yet unborn child would escape the census tax. At that point she spoke, 'Joseph, please hurry.' He immediately supplied the information and promptly paid the tax. Then they were on their way. How can you ever conquer a country when the people laugh at your taxes? I'd give anything to know what happened to that young couple."

"I can tell you," Mordecai responded. "They came to my inn." Artemus looked up in surprise. Mordecai continued. "They came in at the peak of the rush. This young man appeared, pleading for a place for his wife, by now in labor, and himself. I'm not a cruel man, but business is business. I had no room, and even if I had, he couldn't pay what I can ask when there is a crowd in town. While I was explaining this, they caught my wife's eye. She said she'd work something out and led them away.

"But then as that evening wore on, I sensed something strange going on. My wife, my daughter who was helping, or my servant women would disappear from time to time. And then shortly they'd be there, with smiles for everyone. I was puzzled. I took my wife aside and asked what was going on. She whispered, 'I put the young couple in a corner of one of the caves where we stable the animals. She's delivered a son!' Then I understood where they'd been. About an hour later I stepped outside for a breath of air, and without realizing it, my steps took me toward that cave. I returned often through the night, drawn as if by a magnet.

NEIGHBORS OF THE CHRIST NIGHT

Deep in the shelter
   of the cave,
The ass with drooping head
Stood weary
   in the shadow where
His master's hand had led.

About the manger oxen lay,
Bending a wide-eyed gaze
Upon the little
   new-born Babe,
Half worship, half amaze.

High in the roof
   the doves were set
And cooed there,
   soft and mild,
Yet not so sweet as,
   in the hay,
The Mother to her Child.

The gentle cows
   breathed fragrant breath
To keep Babe Jesus warm,
While loud and clear,
   o'er hill and dale,
The cocks crowed,
   "Christ is born!"

Out in the fields,
    beneath the stars,
The young lambs
    sleeping lay
And dreamed
    that in the manger slept
Another innocent as they.

These were Thy neighbors,
    Christmas Child;
To Thee their love was given,
For in Thy baby face
    there shone
The wonder-light of Heaven.

NORA ARCHIBALD SMITH

I looked for moments to return to the manger, to the quiet power, the love, the peace that was there."

At the word peace Ishmael perked up and eagerly responded. "Yes, that's it," he said, "but it wasn't any ordinary peace. You see, I saw the child, too."

Mordecai and Artemus turned their attention to the Arab shepherd. He began, "I've never believed in spirits or even an unseen God. What I see, that's what I believe! If anyone told me what I'm going to tell you, I'd think he'd gone off, touched in the head. Up on shepherd's hill the other night, it turned day in the middle of the night. All of us were scared, but I wanted to know what was going on, so I looked straight at the light while the others hid their heads. I saw messengers in the light. I heard music. I heard voices, voices talking about not being afraid and about joyous news for all people. Then there was something about a Saviour being born, and the way we'd know it was we'd find a baby in a cave! Then it was over. Well, all of us who were off-duty rushed off. A baby in a cave would be something we could see, something we didn't expect to find. But sure enough, there they were. Just like the messenger had said. You were right, Mordecai. There was peace in that manger. But it wasn't just any kind of peace that folks like you and me can make. I only believe what I can see, and I saw peace in those people!"

Mordecai looked up with amazement. "I thought we were strangers. I only waved you over here because I didn't want to lose your business. But now we are bound together by a story." And he reached out in a three-way, embracing handshake, clutching wrists and arms. It was the warmest expression he had ever made to an Arab or a Roman.

By now the last few remaining lamps were burning out of oil. The inn was practically empty. They rose to go.

"*Pax*," said the Roman. "*Shalom*," said the Jew. "*Salaam*," said the Arab. And for those with ears to hear, there was in and beyond the wind, one last refrain of a song that will never be forgotten: "Glory to God in the highest, and on earth peace, good will toward all."

JESUS' WORLD

Some of the coins exchanged during this time had the likeness of the Roman Emperor on one side. The coins Joseph used probably bore the likeness of Caesar Augustus, the ruler of the Roman Empire. Photo of Roman coins by Richard T. Nowitz.

The distance from Nazareth to Bethlehem is approximately ninety miles.

Mary probably rode a donkey which carried the necessary provisions for the journey. Joseph would have walked the distance.

In ancient Israel, one day's wages equaled one *denarius*, in Roman coinage, or one *drachma*, in Greek coinage.

Although King Herod ruled Judea, he answered to Rome. His ten-year rule was marked by the construction of many palaces, the city of Caesarea and its aqueduct system, and the reconstruction of the Temple in Jerusalem. Photo of aqueducts near Caesarea by Alan and Sandy Carey.

Historians tell us that in Bethlehem there was an inn, called a caravansary. People traveling in caravans stopped at the inn and found a safe place to rest and keep their animals.

Caravans consisted of camels and donkeys, bearing travelers and their possessions, and led by a lone rider on a donkey.

Nazareth was located near several major trade routes; one connected the northern province of Galilee to the the southern province of Judah. Photo of ancient stone roadway in Galilee by Nik Wheeler.

To bake bread for their families while they were traveling, women dug a hole in the ground, kindled a small fire in the hole, and then placed smooth stones on top of the fire. In this way, fresh bread could be baked each day. The photo of the makeshift oven above by Richard T. Nowitz.

On their trip, Joseph and Mary probably carried water in a goatskin bag and food in a straw basket.

The Romans built thousands of miles of roads during their reign over much of Europe and the Middle East. These routes connected Egypt, Mesopotamia, and Asia Minor.

THE INNKEEPER

JEAN JONES ANDERSEN

hat's a poor innkeeper to do? We'd barely enough money to pay the bills and not enough feed for the animals for the winter: I can't be expected to turn aside those who can pay for food and lodging. It's hard to say "no," but I have to be reasonable. I'm in business, after all.

It was a pity about that young couple: I felt bad about that. I could see the woman was far along . . . wouldn't surprise me if she gave birth this very night. But I just can't afford sympathy; once you start that, there's no end to it. No, no, I did the only thing I could, the only reasonable, rational thing. I really had no choice in the matter.

So if what I did was right, how come I can't let go of it? I keep seeing their faces . . . going over the whole scene again and again in my mind. It's like there's something there that's so plain, but I'm just missing it. I must be too tired, going soft in the head, no doubt. Can't begin thinking that way.

"Hey, who are you, wandering around out here in the dark? Oh, it's you again. I thought I said . . .Oh, it really is late for her, isn't it? Well, I'm kind of embarrassed to suggest it, but there is a stable out beyond here, in the side of the hill. And I'll see if I can find a couple of things to make you a little more comfortable. Follow me.

Whatever has gotten into me? What I just did made no sense, but I feel somehow good about it. It goes against all my experience and common sense, but somehow it's right. I don't feel so much that I did a "right thing" as that it just somehow happened through me, in spite of me . . . almost as though I'm the one who got a gift, and I should be giving thanks.

And I don't feel so drained and tied in knots any more. Tired, yes, in fact, very tired. But it feels good, and I think I could sleep now, even right here, near the entrance to the stable . . . so if they want anything, they can find me easily.

THE SAVIOUR

The Saviour must have been
A docile Gentleman
To come so far so cold a Day
For little Fellowmen.

The Road to Bethlehem
Since He and I were Boys
Was leveled,
    but for that 'twould be
A rugged billion Miles.

EMILY DICKINSON

Because of the census, the town of Bethlehem would have been extremely crowded, as depicted in James J. Tissot's JOSEPH SEEKS LODGING AT BETHLEHEM (SuperStock). Caesar Augustus ordered a census to be taken in order to efficiently tax all inhabitants of Roman-governed lands. During the first century, the census was held approximately every fourteen years. People went to their ancestral homes in order to register with the government.

HOW FAR IS IT TO BETHLEHEM?

How far is it to Bethlehem?
   Not very far.
Shall we find the stable-room
   Lit by a star?

Can we see the little Child,
   Is He within?
If we lift the wooden latch
   May we go in?

May we stroke the creatures there,
   Ox, ass, or sheep?
May we peep like them and see
   Jesus asleep?

If we touch His tiny hand
   Will he awake?
Will He know we've come so far
   Just for His sake?

Great Kings have precious gifts,
   And we have naught,
Little smiles and little tears
   Are all we brought.

For all weary children
   Mary must weep.
Here on His bed of straw
   Sleep, children, sleep.

God, in His mother's arms,
   Babies in the byre,
Sleep, as they sleep who find
   Their heart's desire.

FRANCES CHESTERTON

Most of the buildings in Bethlehem were built after Jesus' stay there; however, modern Bethlehem still retains many of the architectural features common to buildings which existed during Jesus' lifetime. The archways and columns of this Bethlehem courtyard are typical of the buildings constructed during the Roman rule of Israel. Photo by Jim Whitmer.

THE NATIVITY

Peace? and to all the world? sure, one,
And He the Prince of peace, hath none.
He travels to be born, and then
Is born to travel more again.
Poor Galilee! thou can'st not be
The place for His Nativity.
His restless mother's called away,
And not delivered, till she pay.

A tax? 'tis so still! we can see
The Church thrive in her misery
And like her head at Bethlehem, rise
When she oppressed with troubles, lies.

Rise? should all fall, we cannot be
In more extremities than He.
Great type of passions! come what will,
Thy grief exceeds all copies still.
Thou cam'st from Heaven to Earth, that we
Might go from Earth to Heaven with Thee.

And though Thou found'st no welcome here,
Thou did'st provide us mansions there.
No swaddling silks Thy limbs did fold,
Though Thou could'st turn Thy rays to gold.
No rockers waited on Thy birth,
No cradles stirred, nor songs of mirth;
But her chaste lap and sacred breast
Which lodged Thee first, did give Thee rest.

But stay: what light is that doth stream,
And drop here in a gilded beam?
It is Thy star runs page and brings
Thy tributary Eastern Kings.
Lord! grant some light to us, that we
May with them find the way to Thee.
Behold what mists eclipse the day:
How dark it is! shed down one ray
To guide us out of this sad night,
And say once more, "Let there be light."

HENRY VAUGHAN

A CHILD IS BORN

Fall on your knees, Oh, hear
the angel voices! O night divine,
O night when Christ was born!
O night, O holy night,
O night divine!

THE BIRTH OF CHRIST

nd so it was, that, while they were there, the days were accomplished that she should be delivered. And she brought forth her firstborn son, and wrapped him in swaddling clothes, and laid him in a manger; because there was no room for them in the inn (*Luke 2:6–7*). And he called his name JESUS (*Matthew 1:25*).

In him was life, and the life was the light of men. And the Word was made flesh, and dwelt among us, (and we beheld his glory, the glory as of the only begotten of the Father,) full of grace and truth (*John 1:4, 14*).

In a dream, the angel of the Lord told Joseph that his Child was to be named Jesus. The name Jesus is the Greek form of the name "Joshua," which means "Yahweh is my salvation." Friedrich Sustris's THE ADORATION OF THE SHEPHERDS (Christie's Images/SuperStock) depicts the manger where the Baby Jesus was first laid.

THE CRADLE

CAROL BESSENT HAYMAN

oseph's hands worked the rough wood as he thought back over the events of the past few months. Mary, his betrothed, was with child. His hands trembled as he recalled how she had told him of the visitation of an angel announcing the coming of this Child, a Son—the Son of God, the Saviour of the world!

For days Joseph wrestled with the problem and decided to break the engagement. Then one night the angel of the Lord appeared to him and said Mary had been chosen to bear this Child, God's Son, and that he, Joseph, must accept this miracle of miracles and make Mary his wife.

The cradle frame was smooth now, and his fingers touched it as if in question. What could he use as a design on this cradle, the symbol of his acceptance that the angel's instructions were God's will? He skillfully drew the blade across the wood until a sunburst appeared, radiating from the headpiece. The angel had said that Jesus, the expected Child, would be the "light of the world." This was indeed a fitting symbol for God's Son and for his own amazed and reluctant acceptance of the miracle. He worked to finish the cradle and prepare for the coming journey to Bethlehem to be enrolled by the Roman emperor.

The star burned brightly above the plains of Nazareth as Joseph led the donkey through the narrow cobblestone streets to Mary's house. He helped her up on the donkey. She moved slowly, heavy with the weight of the Child.

Joseph plodded steadily onward, setting a pace that would give him time for his thoughts. The cradle was finished. It lay wrapped in oiled cloths in the corner of the house they would occupy on their return. Of all the pieces of furniture he had made, this was the best. Even now his spirits lifted at the remembrance of the beauty of it. His hands were not those of a skilled artisan, but he had poured all his craftsmanship into it and especially the beautifully carved sunburst headpiece.

CRADLE HYMN

Hush, my dear, lie still
   and slumber;
Holy angels guard thy bed!
Heavenly blessings
   without number
Gently falling on thy head.

Sleep, my babe; thy food
   and raiment,
House and home thy
   friends provide;
All without thy care
   or payment,
All thy wants are
   well supplied.

How much better
   thou'rt attended
Than the Son of God
   could be,
When from Heaven
   He descended,
And became a child
   like thee!

Soft and easy is thy cradle;
Coarse and hard thy
   Saviour lay,
When His birth-place was
   a stable,
And His softest bed was hay.

ISAAC WATTS

Mary and Joseph may have passed through Jerusalem on their way to Bethlehem for the census. They may have passed beneath Zion Gate on their way out of the city. Zion Gate is also called David's Gate because it is closest to the Tomb of David. Photo of Zion Gate by Richard T. Nowitz.

82 🎵 O HOLY NIGHT

CRADLE HYMN

Away in a manger,
No crib for a bed,
The little Lord Jesus
Lay down His sweet head.
The stars in the bright sky
Looked down where He lay,
The little Lord Jesus
Asleep on the hay.

The cattle are lowing,
The baby awakes,
But little Lord Jesus,
No crying He makes.
I love Thee, Lord Jesus!
Look down from the sky,
And stay by my cradle
Till morning is nigh.

MARTIN LUTHER

Giovanni B. S. Sassoferrato's MADONNA WITH THE INFANT JESUS SLEEPING *(Musee du Louvre/Super-Stock) depicts Jesus and His mother. Mary was present for Jesus' first miracle at the wedding feast in Cana and for His crucifixion and resurrection in Jerusalem.*

"Fit for a King." The words forced their way into his mind.

As they neared Bethlehem, Mary grew more tired, and dark circles appeared around her eyes. Joseph hoped to cheer her by telling her of the cradle he had made for the Child. But as the people pressed forward, eager to get the journey over, the little group fell behind, and it was all Joseph could do to guide the tired donkey and keep the rising dust from choking him.

Leading the donkey, Joseph made his way through the crowded streets of Bethlehem. Mary grew more weary, and Joseph, confused and tired, thought of the comfortable room in Nazareth and the beautiful cradle ready to receive the Child. They knocked on many doors, but there was nowhere to stay. Joseph grew concerned as the hours stretched on.

Finally, at the end of the lane, there were lights and the sound of laughter—an inn! He met with the same story, "No room." He gazed beyond the doorway at the crowd. Surely, if this Child Mary carried was God's Son, a place would be provided for His birth? Mary's beseeching look was not lost on the innkeeper's wife nor was the evident tiredness of the donkey. A spark of sympathy crept into her eyes, and she motioned her burly husband aside. "The stable," she said. "The stable is large enough for these."

After they found a place among the beasts, Mary looked up and saw the huge star, so close it seemed to almost hang suspended above them. A song, soft and clear, came from nowhere, and she felt the Child move to enter the world. They swaddled the tiny Babe and looked about for a bed. Joseph thought of the cradle waiting in Nazareth. Suddenly, a light illuminated the stable and settled on the manger, old and worn and filled with fresh hay for the animals. It was to be the cradle of the King. Joseph bowed before the knowledge that Jehovah is God and Christ is God's Son; and they laid Him in a manger.

Suddenly, the voices of angels filled the air, "Glory to God in the highest, and on earth peace, goodwill toward men." Joseph's heart sang with the angels, seeing Mary and the sweet Babe in the manger, the Cradle of God.

CHRIST'S NATIVITY

Awake, glad heart! Get up and sing,
It is the birthday of thy King,
    Awake! awake!
    The sun doth shake
Light from His locks, and all the way,
Breathing perfumes doth spice the day.

Awake! awake! Hark, how th' wood rings,
Winds whisper, and the busy springs
    A consort make;
    Awake! awake!
Man is their high-priest and should rise
To offer up the sacrifice.

I would I were some bird or star,
Flutt'ring in woods or lifted far
    Above this inn
    And road of sin!
Then either star or bird should be
Shining or singing still to Thee.

I would I had in my best part
Fit rooms for Thee, or that my heart
    Were so clean as
    Thy manger was.
But I am all filth and obscene,
Yet, if Thou wilt, Thou canst make clean.

Sweet Jesu! will then; Let no more
This leper haunt and soil Thy door,
    Cure him, ease him
    O release him!
And let once more by mystic birth
The Lord of life be borne in Earth.

HENRY VAUGHAN

*The dawn breaks over Bethlehem, the "city of David"
(Luke 2:4). Photo of Bethlehem by Don North.*

CHRISTMAS LEGENDS

Christmas morn, the legends say,
Even the cattle kneel to pray,
Even the beasts of wood and field
Homage to Christ the Saviour yield.

Horse and cow and woolly sheep
Wake themselves from their heavy sleep,
Bending heads and knees to Him
Who came to earth in a stable dim.

Far away in the forest dark,
Creatures timidly wake and hark;
Feathered bird and furry beast
Turn their eyes to the mystic east.

Loud at the dawning, chanticleer
Sounds his note the rest of the year;
But Christmas Eve the whole night long
Honoring Christ he sings his song.

Christmas morn, the legends say,
Even the cattle kneel to pray,
Even the wildest beast afar
Knows the light of the Saviour's star.

And shall we, for whom He came,
Be by the cattle put to shame?
Shall we not do so much at least
As the patient ox or the forest beast?

Christmas morn, oh, let us sing
Honor and praise to Christ the King,
Sheltered first in a lowly shed,
And cradled there where the cattle fed.

DENIS A. MCCARTHY

Jesus was born in a stable where donkeys, like this one, were fed and kept. Mary may have ridden a similar donkey during her journey to Bethlehem. Photo by Superstock.

HERE AT THE STABLE DOOR

Quick now—loose it—here at the stable door.
Let Christmas winds make sport of this most useless thing,
Tatter it blithesomely, blow it afar.
Be quick: You will not need it any more.

Not if you come inside: pride has no jot
Of relevancy here; it makes no sense
In terms of song or shed, angel or kine—
It has no truck with hay; fields loathe pretense.

Cast it away; lose it in depths of snow
Or in this night's munificence of stars:
You cannot find a single use for pride
Here where the Highest chooses to be low.

M. PAULINUS

THE CHRISTMAS SILENCE

Hushed are the pigeons cooing low,
    On dusty rafters of the loft;
    And mild-eyed oxen, breathing soft,
Sleep on the fragrant hay below.

Dim shadows in the corner hide;
    The glimmering lantern's rays are shed
    Where one young lamb just lifts his head,
Then huddles 'gainst his mother's side.

Strange silence tingles in the air;
    Through the half-open door a bar
    Of light from one low hanging star
Touches the baby's radiant hair—

No sound—the mother, kneeling, lays
    Her cheek against the little face.
    Oh human love! Oh heavenly grace!
'Tis yet in silence that she prays!

Ages of silence end tonight;
    Then to the long expectant earth
    Glad angels come to greet His birth
In burst of music, love, and light.

MARGARET DELAND

Poets and authors traditionally depict cattle as being witnesses of Jesus' birth. Photo of calf by SuperStock.

A CHRISTMAS CAROL

Before the paling of the stars, before the winter morn,
Before the earliest cock-crow, Jesus Christ was born:
Born in a stable, cradled in a manger,
In the world His hands had made, born a stranger.

Priest and King lay fast asleep in Jerusalem;
Young and old lay fast asleep in crowded Bethlehem.
Saint and Angel, ox and ass, kept a watch together,
Before the Christmas daybreak in the winter weather.

Jesus on His Mother's breast in the stable cold,
Spotless Lamb of God was He, Shepherd of the fold.
Let us kneel with Mary Maid, with Joseph bent and hoary,
With Saint and Angel, ox and ass, to hail the King of Glory.

CHRISTINA ROSSETTI

THE CHRISTMAS STORY

Such common things of everyday
Like lowing cattle, fragrant hay,
Stars flung across a velvet sky,
And shepherds watching night go by.

Such common things, and yet they hold
The greatest story ever told—
The story of a Saviour's birth
And hope for man and peace on earth.

VIRGINIA BLANCK MOORE

JESUS' WORLD

Children were wrapped in swaddling clothes until they were six months old. Mothers believed this would cause their children's limbs to grow straight and strong.

Olive oil was made by crushing olives in a press similar to the one pictured at left. Photo by Richard T. Nowitz.

The name Gabriel, God's chosen messenger, means "mighty one of God."

Stables at that time were usually caves enclosed with a wall of rock or wood. Photo by Priscilla Alexander Eastman.

Swaddling clothes were long five-inch-wide linen strips which a mother tightly wrapped around a baby's body. A newborn may have had two or three yards of swaddling bands wrapped around him.

Jesus was laid in a manger— a feeding trough made of rough-hewn wood or possibly even stones.

Because Greek and Roman cultures had strongly influenced Israel, Jewish babies often received two names—one Hebrew and the other Greek or Roman.

Names given to children at this time were often chosen because of special meaning. Elijah means "My God is Yahweh."

During Jesus' time, newborns were rubbed with salt and oil to prevent infection and then wrapped in swaddling clothes.

Each day, new mothers gently unwound the swaddling clothes from their infants and massaged their babies' limbs with olive oil.

Both Matthew and Luke chronicle Jesus' birth in Bethlehem in the New Testament. Photo of Bethlehem bell tower by Thomas R. Fletcher.

A Hymn for Christmas Day

Christians awake, salute the happy morn
Whereon the Saviour of the world was born!
Rise to adore the mystery of love,
Which hosts of angels chanted from above;

With them the joyful tidings first begun
Of God incarnate and the Virgin's Son;
Then to the watchful shepherds it was told,
Who heard the angelic herald's voice: "Behold!

"I bring good tidings of a Saviour's birth
To you and all the nations upon earth;
This day hath God fulfill'd His promis'd word;
This day is born a Saviour, Christ the Lord.

"In David's City, shepherds, ye shall find
The long-foretold Redeemer of mankind;
Wrapt up in swaddling clothes, the Babe divine
Lies in a manger; this shall be your sign."

He spake, and straightway the celestial choir
In hymns of joy, unknown before, conspire.
The praises of redeeming Love they sung,
And Heaven's whole orb with Hallelujahs rung:

God's highest glory was their anthem still;
Peace upon earth and mutual good will.
To Bethlehem straight the shepherds ran,
To see the wonder God has wrought for man;

And found, with Joseph and the blessed maid,
Her Son, the Saviour, in a manger laid.
Amazed, the wondrous story they proclaim,
The first apostles of His infant fame.

While Mary keeps and ponders in her heart
The heavenly vision which the swains impart,
They to their flocks, still praising God, return,
And their glad hearts within their bosom burn.

Let us, like these good shepherds then, employ
Our grateful voices to proclaim the joy;
Like Mary, let us ponder in our mind
God's wondrous love in saving lost mankind.

Artless and watchful, as these favored swains,
While virgin meekness in the heart remains,
Trace we the Babe, who has retrieved our loss,
From the poor manger to His bitter cross.

Treading His steps, assisted by His grace,
Till man's first heavenly state again takes place;
Then may we hope, the angelic throngs among,
To sing, redeemed, a glad triumphal song.

He that was born upon this joyful day,
Around us all, His glory shall display;
Saved by His love, incessant we shall sing
Of angels, and of angel-men, the King.

JOHN BYROM

The shepherds spent weeks in the fields with their flocks and were seen as socially inferior to the farmers and merchants. Hendrick de Clerck's THE ADORATION OF THE SHEPHERDS (Christie's Images/SuperStock) shows the shepherds' wonder and happiness at the Saviour's birth.

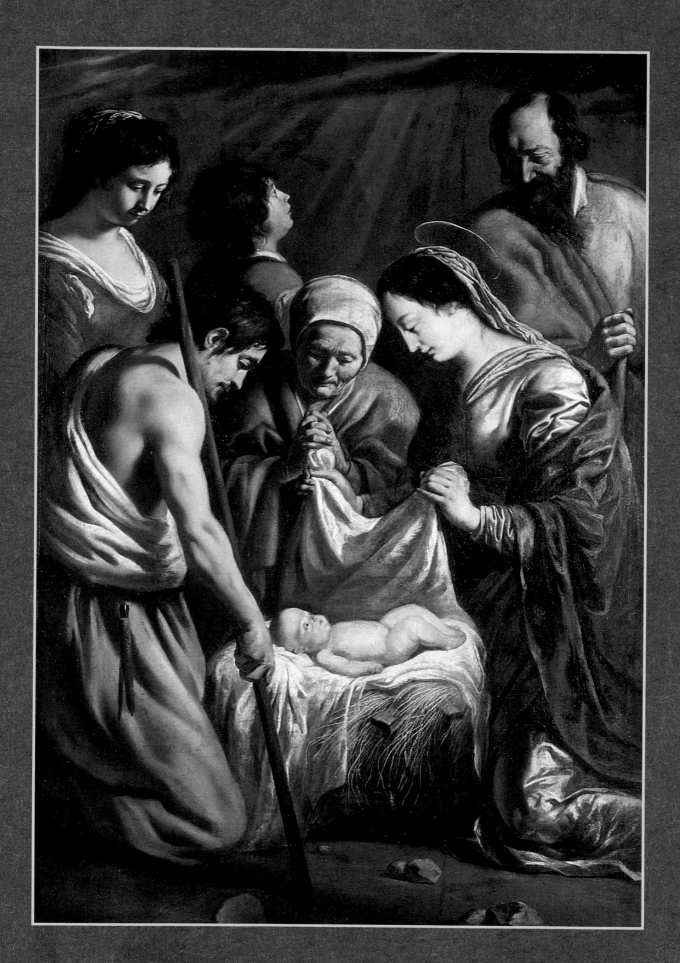

CHRISTMASTIDE

Love came down at Christmas,
  Love all lovely,
    Love Divine;
Love was born at Christmas,
Star and Angels gave the sign.

Worship we the Godhead,
  Love Incarnate,
    Love Divine;
Worship we our Jesus:
But wherewith for sacred sign?

Love shall be our token,
  Love be yours and
    Love be mine,
Love to God and all men,
Love for plea and gift and sign.

CHRISTINA ROSSETTI

Louis Le Nain's THE ADORATION OF
THE SHEPHERDS *(Musee du
Louvre/SuperStock) shows how the
shepherds left their flocks in the fields
and traveled into Bethlehem in order
to find Baby Jesus.*

SHEPHERDS AT THE BACK DOOR

FULTON J. OURSLER

Mary had fallen asleep, and Jesus lay asleep in his first bed, the food box of the donkeys and the cows hastily filled with fresh hay and barley oats that smelled sweet and clean.

For Joseph, sleep was impossible. His mind, his very soul, was too tremulous and excited. "The oddest thing about it," he told himself, in the absence of any companion, "was the feeling I had when I looked into that little fellow's eyes. I seemed to have known Him all my life. He wasn't a stranger!"

Was that a special fact because Jesus was a special child? Because, after all, Joseph was not the child's father, and even now he did not allow himself to forget it. Yet he felt a tender closeness to the baby, deeper and truer than fatherhood itself. He still felt baffled that there was no further sign.

A long time had passed while Mary carried her baby, with no reassurance from supernatural beings. Was it not strange that the baby had been born without some demonstration? Here was the child; where were the angels?

He listened for a rustling of wings and heard only the sleepy bleat of a yearling lamb. That, and presently a low rumble of distant voices, the shuffling of feet outside the house and, at the lower back entrance of the stable, the knocking of a staff. With a gasp of concern that Mary would be awakened, Joseph hurried to the door.

"Peace!" breathed Joseph. "This is no time to make noise."

"The Lord be unto you," returned one of the men in a low, placating voice. "We have not come to make any trouble at all. We are shepherds from the hills outside this town."

"The hour is late," insisted Joseph firmly.

"Wait. Only one question. Has a child just been born in this place?"

A quiver of alarm passed through Joseph. "Why do you

ask, shepherd? How is it your business about a child?"

"Don't be afraid of us, man. We are friends."

"Well, then, yes. A child has been born here."

Low exclamations came from the bearded mouths of the shepherds and one of them whispered, "It is true, then."

And the first speaker laid a kindly hand on Joseph's shoulder, "Tell me—is it a man-child?"

"It is."

"And you have laid the child in a manger?"

"Yes," answered Joseph, feeling the tears gather in his eyes. "There was no cradle, you see. The town is overcrowded; there was nowhere else I could take my wife."

"Then God be praised!" murmured the shepherd fervently, and the others muttered agreement in their beards.

"Listen, man," cried the one with the lifted staff. "We five men have just seen a marvelous sight. An unbelievable sight. And it has to do with you."

Marvelous sight! And unbelievable. Hope sprang up in Joseph's thoughts.

"Believe this thing we tell you. We were tending our flocks tonight. The night was clear, air cool, stars bright, everything going along just as usual. Suddenly Jonas here interrupted our talk and pointed at the sky."

"That I did," confirmed Jonas. "There was a great big bright light in the sky and the shape of it like an angel bigger than the world. And I heard a voice."

"We all saw the light," declared the first man. "And we all heard distinctly that voice from the sky."

"What did the voice say?" asked Joseph eagerly.

"It told us not to be afraid. And then it said it brought us great news. The Savior of the world was being born. I remember the very words; how can I ever forget them? 'For this day is born to you a Saviour who is Christ the Lord'."

"Christ the Lord," whispered Joseph.

"Yes. That's what the voice said. It told us the Child was being born right here in this town and that we would find Him, wrapped in swaddling clothes and lying in a manger."

Here another shepherd pushed himself forward. "You

NEW PRINCE, NEW POMP

Behold a tiny, tender Babe
In freezing winter night,
In homely manger
   trembling lies;
Alas! a piteous sight.

The inns are full; no man
   will yield
This little Pilgrim bed,
But forced He is with silly beasts
In crib to shroud His head.

Despise Him not for lying there,
First, what He is inquire:
An orient pearl is often found
In depth of dirty mire.

Weigh not His crib, His
   wooden dish,
Nor beasts that by Him feed;

Weigh not His mother's
    poor attire,
Nor Joseph's simple weed.

This stable is a Prince's court,
The crib His chair of state;
The beasts are parcel of
    His pomp,
The wooden dish His plate.

The persons in that poor attire
His royal liveries wear;
The Prince Himself is come
    from heaven.
This pomp is prizèd there.

With joy approach,
    O Christian wight,
Do homage to thy King;
And highly prize His
    humble pomp,
Which He from heaven
    doth bring.

ROBERT SOUTHWELL

can never imagine what happened then," he broke in excit-
edly. "The whole heaven seemed to open up. The curtain of
the stars was split like a tent, and through the opening we
saw a host of angels that filled the sky and they were all
singing at the top of their voices."

"And do you know what they were singing?" demanded
Jonas, again interrupting. "The words were: 'Glory to God
in the highest and on earth peace'."

And then the shepherds seemed to loose their tongues.
The sound of their own story seemed to subdue them.
Strong, out-of-doors men, who smelled of grass; practical
men, and yet they had told the story with something of the
frenzy of poets. Now came the reaction.

Their leader lowered his lantern and sighed deeply. "Of
course," he said with an apologetic air, "we can't expect you
to believe all this." Then his eyes flashed open, and he
looked straight at Joseph. "But it is true," he averred, as if
he were taking an oath, "I saw it. I heard it."

Joseph wrung their hands. He believed them utterly, as
they went on to tell how they forsook their fat-tailed sheep
and ran into Bethlehem. Of every dark straggler on the
streets at such an hour they had asked questions. Where
could they find the newborn baby? Someone had sent them
to the stable of the inn.

The tale of the shepherds brought peace to Joseph. The
sign had come secondhand, which was better. These men,
panting and out of breath and sweaty, full of strength and
humility, had seen the gates of another world open up and
had heard singing from on high, the heavens rejoicing at
the birth. Humble workingmen of the fields were the first
to come and visit the newborn Jesus.

Joseph received them with open arms. On tiptoe they
followed him as he led them straight to the manger, where
they knelt beside the sleeping figure of Mary's son.

Soon they were gone, and Joseph resumed his vigil. But
now his heart was calmed. The sign had come. In his mind's
ear he could hear the unnumbered hosts of the servants of
God singing: "Peace on earth to men of good will."

THE SHEPHERDS AND ANGELS

Led by the light of faith serenely
beaming, with glowing hearts by
His cradle we stand.

THE ANGELS APPEAR TO THE SHEPHERDS

And there were in the same country shepherds abiding in the field, keeping watch over their flock by night. And, lo, the angel of the Lord came upon them, and the glory of the Lord shone round about them: and they were sore afraid.

And the angel said unto them, Fear not: for, behold, I bring you good tidings of great joy, which shall be to all people. For unto you is born this day in the city of David a Saviour, which is Christ the Lord.

And this shall be a sign unto you; Ye shall find the babe wrapped in swaddling clothes, lying in a manger.

And suddenly there was with the angel a multitude of the heavenly host praising God and saying, Glory to God in the highest, and on earth peace, good will toward men.

And it came to pass, as the angels were gone away from them into heaven, the shepherds said one to another, Let us now go even unto Bethlehem, and see this thing which is come to pass, which the Lord hath made known unto us.

And they came with haste, and found Mary, and Joseph, and the babe lying in a manger.

And when they had seen it, they made known abroad the saying which was told them concerning this child. And all they that heard it wondered at those things which were told them by the shepherds. But Mary kept all these things, and pondered them in her heart.

And the shepherds returned, glorifying and praising God for all the things that they had heard and seen, as it was told unto them (*Luke 2:8–20*).

Upon seeing the angels and hearing their loud praises, the shepherds immediately left their sheep and sought out the Christ Child. In Joseph Heintz's THE ADORATION OF THE SHEPHERDS (Christie's Images/SuperStock), we see the joy of these rough men, men who became evangelists when they "made known" the birth of the Messiah, Jesus Christ.

FROM PARADISE REGAINED

At Thy nativity
   a glorious choir
Of Angels in the fields
   of Bethlehem sung
To shepherds, watching
   at their folds by night
And told them
   the Messiah now was born,
Where they might see Him;
   and to Thee they came,
Directed to the manger
   where Thou lay'st,
For in the inn
   was left no better room.

A star, not seen before,
   in heaven appearing,
Guided the wise men thither
   from the East,
To honor Thee with incense,
   myrrh, and gold;
By whose bright course
   led on they found the place,
Affirming it Thy star,
   new-graven in heaven,
By which they knew Thee,
   King of Israel born.

     JOHN MILTON

The "multitude of heavenly host" that rejoiced at Jesus' birth and praised God may have appeared similar to the angels in this detail from Antonio Maria Viani's TRINITY WITH SAINTS URSULA AND MARGARET (Palazzo Ducale/SuperStock).

ANGELS AND SHEPHERDS

DENIS O'SHEA

 n the night of the first Christmas Eve, the rocky hillock was enveloped in darkness. At its base there was a crescent-shaped cavern with a wide mouth facing north, making it well lighted by day. It was approached by a gentle ascent from the fields below. The tower on the summit of the rock commanded an extensive view of the surrounding sheep walks. The long, open front of the cavern was protected by the customary stone wall, and the entrance could have been enclosed with a gate or, more likely, with a pile of thorn bushes.

The traditional number of the shepherds on guard is three, and all would be within the fold, for the darkness of night would not warrant stationing a man in the watch-tower. As the night was cold, they would have lighted a fire from a pile of thorny brushwood. Behold them, squatting around their fire in the cavern, warming their bare legs, with their rough sheepskin mantles worn with the fleece next to the body pulled closely around their shoulders, and their staffs and slings laid close at hand, ready to start up at the first hint of danger. Their unkempt, shaggy dogs lay at their feet near the thorn-filled gap, blinking their eyes in the light of the fire, but with ears alert to catch the first sound of danger.

The sheep filled the rest of the commodious cavern. There were no lambs as yet in the flock for it was too early for the lambing season. It is easy to picture this pastoral scene in the cavern: the shepherds chatting or dozing over the fire with their dogs at their feet, and the white mass of animals behind in the darkness, snug, warm, and sheltered from wind and rough weather. Outside all was dark and still. Within the cave the firelight flickered on the smoke-blackened walls and the many rounded backs of the sheep.

We are told that the angel "came upon them." The shepherds' first intimation of his presence was his appearance as the "the glory of the Lord shone round about them," in such a blaze of celestial splendor that darkness seemed turned into daylight. This brilliance was not evanescent like a flash of lightning but as steady as the noonday sun. The red, leaping flame of their fire seemed to sink and fade as if strong sunlight beat upon it. Every stone in the rough wall of the fold and every tuft of wool upon the backs of the sheep seemed to stand out distinctly. The shepherds suddenly looked up to find an angel of God standing beside them in the cavern. No wonder they feared as they looked upon him, glorious and beautiful, the messenger of the Most High.

Being a pure spirit, the angel had to assume some bodily form in order to become visible to mortal eyes. Like other angels upon previous manifestations, he probably took a human form and appeared like a man. Abraham and Manoah had mistaken angels for mere men.

Wild, ignorant men though they were, the shepherds could not misunderstand the significance of the phrase "Christ the Lord," for the words were a popular description of the expected Messiah. Besides, this was Bethlehem, the city of David, the very place where He was expected to be born. Good tidings, great news indeed, the very best they had ever heard! Now they understood why the skies without were illuminated, and that the great being beside them was the herald of His Master.

The shepherds looked out of their folds and saw, not one, but thousands of angels. Heaven's own choir turned out to sing the carol of a Child cradled in a manger! Over the snow-clad fields below, over the hill of Mar Elias that intervened and hid Jerusalem from them, they saw the hosts of heaven deploy their brilliant ranks. The whole landscape was lit up with the splendor of legions of angels. Over the Flock Tower above their heads, over the bare fields, over the flat roofs of the town, over the hills of Bethlehem circled the glittering choirs of heaven, and the voices of angels sang the

ANGELS FROM THE REALMS OF GLORY

Angels, from the realms
   of glory,
Wing your flight o'er all
   the earth;
Ye who sang creation's story,
Now proclaim the
   Messiah's birth:

Come and worship,
   Come and worship,
Worship Christ,
   the newborn King.

Shepherds in the
   fields abiding,
Watching o'er your flocks
   by night,
God with man is
   now residing;
Yonder shines the
   infant Light.

Come and worship,
   Come and worship,
Worship Christ,
   the newborn King.

JAMES MONTGOMERY

Shepherd's Fields outside Bethlehem remain as calm as during Christ's lifetime. The life of a shepherd, however, was not always tranquil. Shepherds lived out in the elements, drove off bandits and animals, nursed sick animals, moved constantly to find suitable grazing and water for their herds, and spent many days alone. Abel, Abraham, Moses, David, and Amos were all shepherds. Photo of Shepherd's Field by Priscilla Alexander Eastman.

triumphant strains of "*Gloria in excelsis Deo!*"

The presence of the angels was as real as the presence of the shepherds. In Bethlehem two worlds met—the supernatural and the natural, and one was as real as the other. The invisible King of the unseen realms of heaven took a visible form upon earth, and hosts of His heavenly creatures came visibly to adore Him. After the birth itself, no incident of that memorable night has so impressed the minds of Christians as the rush of the angels over the fields of Bethlehem. Historically the supernatural is as much a part of the scene as the natural. Our view of the picture becomes wrong, incomplete, out of focus if we have eyes for the natural alone. The appearance upon earth of God's heavenly creatures is less a wonder than the coming of God Himself.

HOW GRAND AND HOW BRIGHT

How grand and how bright that wonderful night
    When angels to Bethlehem came;
They burst forth like fires, and they shot their loud lyres
    And mingled their sound with the flame.

The Shepherds were amazed, the pretty lambs gazed
    At darkness thus turned into light;
No voice was there heard from man, beast, nor bird,
    So sudden and solemn the sight.

And then when the sound re-echoed around,
    The hills and the dales awoke;
The moon and the stars stopped their fiery cars
    And listened while Gabriel spoke.

I bring you, said he, from that glorious tree
    A message both gladsome and good;
Our Saviour is come to the world as His home,
    But He lies in a manger of wood.

At mention of this, the source of all bliss,
    The angels sang loudly and long;
They soared to the sky beyond mortal eye,
    But left us the words of their song.

AUTHOR UNKNOWN

This detail from G. Battista Caporali's THE NATIVITY WITH
MUSIC-MAKING ANGELS ABOVE, THE ANNUNCIATION TO THE
SHEPHERDS BEYOND *(Christie's Images/SuperStock) points to the
heavenly revelry which echoed through the hills outside Bethlehem.
Undoubtedly, the angels' praises were among the most joyful noises
heard on earth.*

Jesus' World

Shepherds were seen as part of the lower class because their work prevented them from keeping the ceremonial Levitical laws as they moved about the countryside tending their flocks. They were considered unreliable, and it was common for them to be regarded as thieves. Shepherds were not allowed to give evidence in the courts.

Most shepherds wore an unbleached cotton shirt, a leather girdle, and a wool cloak which also served as a blanket.

Caves in the hills of Bethlehem provided shepherds safe havens for their sheep during the night. The sheep were counted as they went into the caves in the evening and counted again as they departed in the morning. Photo by Anthony R. Dalton.

In the Bible, the apostle Paul says to offer all people hospitality because "some have entertained angels unawares" (*Hebrews 13:2*).

Flocks of goats and sheep still graze in the rugged mountains of Israel much as they did during Jesus' time. Photo by Galyn C. Hammond.

Because angels bring messages from God, the Bible exhorts people to listen to the message of an angel, "Beware of him, and obey his voice, provoke him not" (*Exodus 23:21*), but not to worship an angel because he is "a fellow-servant" (*Revelation 19:10, 22:9*).

In the Bible, angels' appearances sometimes inspire awe and fear. When Zacharias first saw the angel Gabriel in the Temple, he was consumed with fear, and as soon as Manoah and his wife realized they had been in the presence of the angel of the Lord, they "fell on their faces to the ground" and felt they would "surely die" (*Judges 13:20, 22*).

The angel Gabriel is mentioned in the Book of Daniel and in the Gospel of Luke. In art Gabriel is often portrayed as a benevolent figure.

Livestock stables are still built from the rocks found in the fields around Bethlehem, just as they were in Jesus' time. Photo by Anthony R. Dalton.

The cherubim and seraphim mentioned in the Bible possibly refer to types or classes of angels.

Gabriel and Michael are the only named angels in the Bible. Michael appears in the Books of Daniel, Jude, and Revelation.

Sheep and shepherds are mentioned over 300 times in the Bible. Photo by Lior Rubin.

MICHAEL AND THE SHEPHERD

ELIZABETH GOUDGE

ood evening," said David politely, edging a little closer. "'Tis a fine evening, but cold about the legs."

"Is it? Then come under my cloak," said the stranger, lifting it so that it suddenly seemed to spread about him like great wings, and David, all his fear suddenly evaporated, scuttled forward and found himself gathered in against the stranger's side, under the stranger's cloak, warm and protected and sublimely happy.

"But where are the others?" he asked. "Eli and Jacob and Tobias?"

"They've gone to Bethlehem," said the stranger. "They've gone to a birthday party."

"A birthday party, and didn't take me?" ejaculated David in powerful indignation. "The nasty, selfish brutes!"

"They were in rather a hurry," explained the stranger. "It was all rather unexpected."

"Then I suppose they had no presents to take?" asked David. "They'll feel awkward turning up with no presents. Serve them right for not taking me."

"They took what they could," said the stranger. "A shepherd's crook, a cloak, and a loaf of bread."

David snorted with contempt, and then snorted again in indignation. "They shouldn't have gone," he said, and indeed it was a terrible crime for shepherds to leave their sheep, with those robbers prowling about in the shadows below and only too ready to pounce upon them.

"They were quite right to go," said the stranger. "And I have taken their place."

"But you're only one man," objected David, "and it takes several to tackle robbers."

"I think I'm equal to any number of robbers," smiled the

THE SHEPHERD BOY

Like some vision olden
Of far other time,
When the age was golden,
In the young world's prime
Is thy soft pipe ringing,
O lonely shepherd boy.

What song art thou singing,
In thy youth and joy?
Or art thou complaining
Of thy lowly lot;
And thine own disdaining
Dost ask what thou hast not?
Of the future dreaming,
Weary of the past,
For the present scheming,
All but what thou hast.

No, thou art delighting
In thy summer home,
Where the flowers inviting
Tempt the bee to roam;
Where the cowslip bending,
With its golden bells,
Of each glad hour's ending
With a sweet chime tells.

All wild creatures love him
When he is alone,
Every bird above him
Sings its softest tone.
Thankful to high Heaven,
Humble in thy joy,
Much to thee is given,
Lowly shepherd boy.

LETITIA ELIZABETH LANDON

The fields pictured are similar to the ones where Ruth, the daughter-in-law of Naomi, gleaned barley from Boaz's fields. Boaz and Ruth are listed in Jesus' lineage. Photo of shepherd in fields outside Bethlehem by SuperStock.

stranger. He was making a statement, not boasting, and David thrilled to the quiet confidence of his voice, and thrilled, too, to feel the strength of the arm that was round him and of the knee against which he leant.

"Have you done a lot of fighting, great lord?" he whispered in awe.

"Quite a lot," said the stranger.

"Who did you fight?" breathed David. "Barbarians?"

"The devil and his angels," said the stranger nonchalantly.

David was momentarily deprived of the power of speech, but pressing closer he gazed upward at the face of this man for whom neither robbers nor devils seemed to hold any terrors, and once he began to look he could not take his eyes away, for never before had he seen a face like this man's, a face at once delicate and strong, full of power yet quick with tenderness, bright as the sky in early morning yet shadowed with mystery. It seemed an eternity before David could find his voice.

"Who are you, great lord?" he whispered at last. "You're no shepherd."

"I'm a soldier," said the stranger. "And my name is Michael. . . . What's your name?"

"David," murmured the little boy, and suddenly he shut his eyes because he was dazzled by the face above him. If this was a soldier, he was a very king among soldiers.

"Tell me where you are going, David," said the stranger.

Now that they had told each other their names David felt they were lifelong friends, and it was not hard to tell his story. He told it all; his father's illness, his mother's tears, the children's hunger, the cold home where there was no fire and the oil was nearly finished; and his longing to be a rich man that he might help them all.

"But I hadn't meant to go down to the road alone, you see," he finished. "I thought Eli would have gone with me, and now Eli has gone to that birthday party."

"Then you'll have to go alone," said Michael.

"I suppose the sheep wouldn't be all right by themselves?" hinted David gently.

"They certainly would not," said Michael firmly.

CHRISTMAS HYMN

In the fields with their
    flocks abiding,
They lay on the
    dewy ground;
And glimmering under
    the starlight,
The sheep lay white around,
When the light of the Lord
    streamed o'er them,
And lo! from the
    heaven above,
An angel leaned from
    the glory
And sang his song of love.
He sang, that first
    sweet Christmas,
The song that shall
    never cease:
"Glory to God in
    the highest,
On earth good will
    and peace."

"To you in the City of David
    A Saviour is born to-day!"
And suddenly a host
    of the heavenly ones
Flashed forth to join the lay!
O never hath
    sweeter message
Thrilled home to the souls
    of men,

And the heavens themselves
    had never heard
A gladder choir till then,
For they sang that
    Christmas carol
That never on earth
    shall cease:
"Glory to God in the highest,
On earth good will
    and peace."

And the shepherds came to
    the manger
And gazed on the
    Holy Child;
And calmly o'er that
    rude cradle,
The Virgin Mother smiled;
And the sky in the
    star-lit silence
Seemed full of the angel lay:
"To you in the City of David
    A Saviour is born to-day."
O, they sang—and I know
    that never
The carol on earth
    shall cease:
"Glory to God in the highest,
On earth good will
    and peace."

FREDERICK WILLIAM FARRAR

"I'm not afraid, of course," boasted David, and shrank a little closer against that strong knee.

"Of course not," concurred Michael heartily. "I've noticed that Davids are always plucky. Look at King David fighting the lion and the bear when he was only a shepherd boy like you."

"But the Lord God Jehovah guided and protected him," said David.

"And the Lord God will protect you," said Michael.

"I don't *feel* as though He was protecting me," objected David.

"You haven't started out yet," said Michael, and laughed. "How can He protect you when there's nothing to protect you from? Or guide you when you don't take to the road? Go on now. Hurry up."

And with a gentle but inexorable movement he withdrew his knee from beneath David's clinging hands, and lifted his cloak from David's shoulders so that it slid back with a soft rustling upward movement, as though great wings were folded against the sky. And the winter wind blew cold and chill about the little boy who stood ragged and barefoot in the blackness of the night.

"Good-bye," said Michael's deep voice; but it seemed to be drifting away as though Michael too were withdrawing himself. "Play your pipe to yourself if you are afraid, for music is the voice of man's trust in God's protection, even as the gift of courage is God's voice answering."

David took a few steps forward, and again terror gripped him. Again he saw the bare lonely hills, and the shadows down below where the robbers lurked. He glanced back over his shoulder, ready to bolt back to the shelter of Michael's strong arm and the warmth of his cloak. But he could no longer see Michael very clearly, he could only see a dark shape that might have been a man but that might have been only a shadow. But yet the moment he glanced back he knew that Michael was watching him, Michael the soldier who was afraid neither of robbers nor of the devil and his angels, and with a heart suddenly turned valiant he turned and scuttled off down the hill toward the valley.

THE NEW DOCTRINE

Ye shepherds! angels now!
  who gladly heard
That midnight Word of God
  in music given,
Which told of Christ's Nativity
  and stirr'd
Your hearts with melodies
  from middle heaven,
Tend this poor creedless youth
  through David's town!
Be ever near him
  with a silent spell
And lead him to the spot
  where, floating down
Upon your watch,
  the choral blessing fell!
There charm away his false
  and flimsy lore
And breathe into his soul
  your simple creed,
The child of angels' hymns
  and good men's heed,
The faith of Jesus Christ,
  nor less nor more—
So may he all his erring
  steps retrace
And bless sweet Bethlehem
  for her day of grace.

CHARLES TENNYSON TURNER

*Pedro Garcia de Benabarre's THE
ANNUNCIATION OF SAINT JOACHIM
(Christie's Images) shows the scene that
transpired in the fields outside Bethlehem on a cold, dark night. God sent
His heavenly messengers to announce
His Son's birth with the majesty befit-
ting the arrival of the Prince of Peace
and the King of kings.*

THE SHEPHERD'S STORY

WASHINGTON GLADDEN

ring that sheepskin, Joseph, and lay it down on this bank of dry earth under this shelving rock. The sky is fair and the moon is rising, and we can sit here and watch the flock on the hillside below. Your young blood and your father's coat of skins will keep you warm for one watch. At midnight, my son, your father, and his brother will take our places; for the first watch you and I will tend the sheep."

"You said, Grandfather, that you always spend this night with the flocks in the fields. Why this night?" the boy asked.

"Do you know, my boy, that this is the night of the year on which the Lord Christ was born?"

"Oh yes," answered the lad. "My father told me you were with the sheep that night. How long ago was that, Grandfather?"

"Just fifty years ago this night."

"And how old were you then?"

"Fourteen, and a stout boy for my age. I had been for two years in the fields with my father and had tasted to the full the hardships and dangers of the shepherd's life. My father and his brother James, and Hosea, a neighbor and kinsman of ours, were with me. We had driven forth our flock from Bethlehem and were dwelling by night in the shelter of the tower on the hillside yonder, watching and sleeping, two and two. My father and I were wont to keep the earlier watches. At midnight we would call James and Hosea to relieve us, and they would watch till morning.

"But that night, when the sun went down and the stars came out, we were all sitting here, upon this hillside, talking of the troubles of Israel and the promises of deliverance spoken of by the prophets; and James and Hosea were asking my father questions, and he was answering them, for he

was older than they, and all the people of Bethlehem rever-
enced him as a wise and devout man.

"Suddenly I saw my father rise to his feet. Then the
other men sprang up with astonishment and wonder upon
their faces. It had grown light all at once, lighter than the
brightest moon; and as I turned my face in the direction in
which the others were looking, I saw, standing there upon
that level place, a figure majestic and beautiful beyond the
power of words to describe. My heart stopped beating. The
others were standing, but I had no power to rise. I lay there
motionless upon the earth. My eyes were fixed upon that
wonderful face, upon those clear, shining eyes, upon that
brow that seemed to beam with the purity of the soul
within. It was not a smile with which that face was lighted.
It was something too noble and exalted to call by that
name. It was a look that told of power and peace, of joy and
triumph."

"Did you know that it was an angel?"

"I knew not anything. I only knew what I saw was glorious, too glorious for mortal eyes to look upon. Yet while I
gazed, the terribleness of the look began to disappear, the
sweetness and grace of the soul shone forth, and I had
almost ceased to tremble before the angel opened his
mouth. And when he spoke, his voice, clearer than any
trumpet and sweeter than any lute, charmed away all my
fears.

" 'Be not afraid,' he said, 'for behold I bring you good
tidings of great joy. For there is born to you this day, in the
city of David, a Saviour.'

"Oh, that voice, my boy! It makes my heart beat now to
remember its sweetness. It seemed to carry these words into
our innermost hearts, to print them on our memories, so
that we never could forget one syllable of what he said.
And then he turned aside and lifted his face toward
heaven, and in a tone louder, but yet so sweet that it did
not startle us at all, came forth from his lips the first strain
of that great song: 'Glory to God in the highest!'

"But then came the softer tones, less grand, but even

A PRAYER AT BETHLEHEM

O pulsing earth
   with heart athrill
With infinite
   creative will!

O watchful shepherds
   in whose eyes
Sweet hopes
   and promises arise!

O angel-host
   whose chanting choir
Proclaims fulfillment
   of desire!

O flaming star
   so purely white
Against the black
   Judean night!

O blessed Mary
   bending low
With sense
   of motherhood aglow!

O holy Babe
   with haloed head
Soft pillowed
   in a manger bed!

O Mystery
   divine and deep
Help us
   Thy prophecies to keep!

ANNE P. L. FIELD

Shepherds in Israel did not drive their flocks; instead, they led them and lived close to them, like these shepherds in Shepherd's Field outside Bethlehem. The shepherd's proximity to his fold created a close bond, and each sheep in the flock knew his own shepherd's voice. Jesus used this familiar relationship between sheep and shepherd to teach about the relationship of Christ to His flock. Photo of Shepherd's Field by Dave Bartruff/FPG International.

sweeter, 'Peace on earth, good-will toward men'."

"Did you see the choir of angels overhead?"

"I saw nothing. The brightness was too dazzling for mortal eyes. We all stood there, with downcast eyes, listening spellbound to the wonderful melody until the chorus ceased and the stars came back again.

"The first to break the silence was my father. 'Come,' he said in a solemn voice. 'let us go at once to Bethlehem, and see this thing which is come to pass, which the Lord hath made known unto us'."

THE MAGI

So led by light of a star
sweetly gleaming, here came the
wise men from the Orient land.

THE MAGI
WORSHIP JESUS

ow when Jesus was born in Bethlehem of Judaea in the days of Herod the king, behold, there came wise men from the east to Jerusalem, saying, Where is he that is born King of the Jews? For we have seen his star in the east, and are come to worship him.

When Herod the king had heard these things, he was troubled, and all Jerusalem with him. And when he had gathered all the chief priests and scribes of the people together, he demanded of them where Christ should be born.

And they said unto him, In Bethlehem of Judaea: for thus it is written by the prophet:

And thou Bethlehem, in the land of Judah, art not the least among the princes of Judah: for out of thee shall come a Governor, that shall rule my people Israel.

Then Herod, when he had privily called the wise men, enquired of them diligently what time the star appeared. And he sent them to Bethlehem, and said, Go and search diligently for the young child; and when ye have found him, bring me word again, that I may come and worship him also.

When they had heard the king, they departed; and lo, the star, which they saw in the east, went before them, till it came and stood over where the young child was. When they saw the star, they rejoiced with exceeding great joy.

And when they were come into the house, they saw the young child with Mary his mother, and fell down, and worshiped him: and when they had opened their treasures, they presented unto him gifts; gold, and frankincense, and myrrh (*Matthew 2: 1–11*).

This detail from Hans Memling's SEVEN JOYS OF MARY (Alte Pinakothek/SuperStock) shows the pomp of the Magi's arrival. The Magi traveled from the East in order to see the newborn King of the Jews.

THE HOLY STAR

As shadows cast by cloud
    and sun
Flit o'er the summer grass,
So in Thy sight,
    Almighty One,
Earth's generations pass.

And while the years,
    an endless host,
Come pressing swiftly on,
The brightest names that
    earth can boast
Just glisten and are gone.

Yet doth the Star
    of Bethlehem shed
A lustre pure and sweet,
And still it leads, as once
    it led,
To the Messiah's feet.

O Father, may that holy star
Grow every year more bright
And send its glorious
    beams afar
To fill the world with light.

WILLIAM CULLEN BRYANT

*The Star in the East was specially
sent for the nativity in order to guide
the Magi to Bethlehem. This heavenly phenomenon was surely more
majestic than any comet or other
celestial occurrence we have seen
since, such as the Hale-Bopp comet
pictured here. Photo of the comet by
Greg Voight/International Stock.*

THE EPIPHANY OF THE MAGI

MARJORIE HOLMES

 or forty days the rude little stable was their home. And each night the great star stood over its entrance. Joseph had never seen such a star, flaming now purple, now white, now gold. Its light illuminated the countryside.

Joseph stood one night at the stable door. He had been to the well for water, but he could not go in just yet. The night was cold and clear, it was exhilarating and yet peaceful to stand for a moment before joining his loved ones inside. From this little distance he stood savoring it, the sweet communion of the stable.

Tomorrow they must take the little Jesus and travel to the Temple, there to redeem Him with an offering. After that, Joseph reasoned, it would be well to come back to Bethlehem and find work until the Baby was old enough to attempt the treacherous journey back to Nazareth. "Would the star follow them?" he wondered. "Would it continue to blaze above their heads like a torch to light the way?"

"Where now, star?" he thought. "Guide me, lead me."

Taking up the cool bulging skins, he was about to go in when he heard the pluck of approaching hooves and the jingle of harness, and saw, flowing slowly down the pathway from the inn, three camels. He paused, curiously repelled and attracted by the serpentine necks and undulant heads festooned with tassels, the arrogant grace of them as they moved, and the commanding elegance of their riders. Rich merchants, evidently, dark princes from some far country. And it flashed through his consciousness that it was strange they had not summoned a servant to stable their mounts instead of themselves riding down from the inn.

Joseph turned hastily, not wishing to be seen, and was about to duck into the cave when one of them called out to him. "Wait! You there in the doorway." The camel drew nearer. "Tell me, is this the place where the new Child lies?"

Joseph stood rigid, silent in the grip of a terrible apprehension.

"Of course it is, it has to be." The second rider was making a gesture of triumph toward the star. "See, it no longer moves."

"But, a stable!" The third rider drew abreast. "Surely this is no fit birthplace for a King."

Joseph's heart had begun to beat in heavy strokes. Obviously these were men of travel and learning, men on a vital mission, and he was afraid. A great foreboding rose up in him, and a fierce rebellion. What did such men want with his Child? Were the dread momentous things hinted at so darkly in the prophets already about to begin? He would not have it. Not yet, not yet! The Child was not ready; His little life had only just begun.

He stood blocking the doorway as the strangers prepared to dismount, rapping the growling beasts on the neck so that they folded their thin legs to crouch.

"Why do you ask?" Joseph demanded. "What do you want?"

"To see him. Is there not a newborn child within?"

Joseph hesitated. "Only my wife and Son."

They regarded him. One was tall and handsome, with a curling black beard and teeth that flashed white in his swarthy face. The other two were fairer. All had the look of wisdom and splendor about them, humbling Joseph, a sense of purpose and wills that were not easily to be denied.

"You are the father then? Of this holy Child?"

"My wife has borne a Son," he said. "I am the father of a month old Son. And is not every child sacred in the sight of God?"

"Yes. Yes, truly," said the tall one after a second. "But the stars have foretold this event for years. We have studied the stars. We are Magi from Persia and Chaldea, philosophers and physicians, and we have traveled for weeks following the star that stands over this doorway. It has become

Hymn for the Nativity

Happy night and happy silence
   downward softly stealing,
Softly stealing over land
   and sea;
Stars from golden censors
   swing a silent eager feeling
Down on Judah,
   down on Galilee;
And all the wistful air,
   and earth and sky,
Listened, listened
   for the gladness of a cry.

Holy night, a sudden flash
   of light its way is winging,
Angels, angels,
   all above, around;
Hark, the angel voices, hark,
   the angel voices singing;
And the sheep are lying
   on the ground.
Lo, all the wistful air
   and earth and sky,
Listen, listen
   to the gladness of the cry.

Wide, as if the light were music,
   flashes adoration:
"Glory be to God,
   nor ever cease."
All the silence thrills,
   and speeds the message
   of salvation:

"Peace on earth, good-will to
    men of peace."
Lo, all the wistful air
    and earth and sky,
Listen, listen to the gladness of
    the cry.

Holy night thy solemn
    silence evermore enfoldeth
Angels' songs and peace from
    God on high;
Holy night, thy watcher still
    with faithful eye beholdeth
Wings that wave and angel
    glory nigh.
Lo, hushed is strife in air
    and earth and sky;
Still thy watchers hear
    the gladness of the cry.

Praise Him, ye who watch the
    night, the silent night
    of ages;
Praise Him, shepherds,
    praise the Holy Child;
Praise Him, ye who hear
    the light;
O praise Him, all ye sages;
Praise Him, children, praise
    Him meek and mild.
Lo, peace on earth, glory to
    God on high,
Listen, listen to the gladness of
    the cry.

EDWARD THRING

the sole purpose of our existence, my friend, to see Him, if only for a few minutes, this Child of yours who is to change the course of all history. This one who is to become King of the Jews." The voice was grave, at once stern and imploring, "Surely you would not turn us away?"

Joseph gazed into the stranger's impassioned eyes. And he knew that it was ended, the peaceful dream of the stable with the Child as only a child at its center and heart. For cradled there in the clay manger lay all the portent and promise, the Man of destiny.

"Wait," he said brusquely. "I must go and consult my wife."

"I'm sorry I was gone so long," he said. "But there are strangers at the door insisting they must see Him. They are wise men, Mary, come all the way from Persia and Chaldea, they claim."

Mary gasped. And she too was bewildered and suddenly stricken. "Wise men? Then you must not keep them waiting."

In a few moments she could hear the pound of sandals and the swish of robes as they approached; it was like the ominous rush and pound of some majestic but overpowering sea. They filled the room with their turbaned strangeness, their exotic smell of spices and perfume. But one by one they knelt and gazed long upon the Baby, who smiled at them with His great liquid eyes and strove within His bindings, as if to reach out to them. And they laughed gently, and opening their embroidered shawls, presented their gifts: jars of precious myrrh and frankincense, a bolt of silk shot through with gold, a ruby in a velvet case.

"For the King," they said, rising unsteadily and brushing at their eyes. "For the hope of the ages. And for you, His mother." One of them draped a cashmere shawl about Mary's slight shoulders.

"And you." A leather bag of coins was pressed into Joseph's hand. "Use it to lighten your load. For it is a heavy load you have been elected to carry, and a long journey that you will surely have to make."

BRIGHTEST AND BEST
OF THE SONS OF THE MORNING

Brightest and best of the Sons of the morning!
Dawn on our darkness and lend us thine aid!
Star of the East, the horizon adorning,
Guide where our Infant Redeemer is laid!

Cold on His cradle the dew-drops are shining,
Low lies His head with the beasts of the stall;
Angels adore Him in slumber reclining,
Maker and Monarch and Saviour of all.

Say, shall we yield Him, in costly devotion,
Odors of Edom and offerings divine?
Gems of the mountain and pearls of the ocean,
Myrrh from the forest or gold from the mine?

Vainly we offer each ample oblation,
Vainly with gifts could His favor secure;
Richer by far is the heart's adoration,
Dearer to God are the prayers of the poor.

Brightest and best of the Sons of the morning!
Dawn on our darkness and lend us thine aid!
Star of the East, the horizon adorning,
Guide where our Infant Redeemer is laid!

REGINALD HEBER

Tradition has given the Magi names, although the Bible does not. They are assumed to have been wealthy because of the gifts they brought. They are also assumed to have been kings because they met directly with King Herod. In any event, their visit to the stable must have caused quite a stir. Hieronymus Bosch's ADORATION OF THE MAGI (Bearsted Collection/SuperStock) captures the juxtaposition of the rich noblemen and their humble surroundings.

CHRISTMAS CAROL

The kings, they came from out the south,
All dressed in ermine fine;
They bore Him gold and chrysoprase,
And gifts of precious wine.

The shepherds came from out the north;
Their coats were brown and old;
They brought Him little new-born lambs—
They had not any gold.

The wise men came from out the east,
And they were wrapped in white;
The star that led them all the way
Did glorify the night.

The angels came from heaven high,
And they were clad with wings;
And lo, they brought a joyful song
The host of heaven sings.

The kings, they knocked upon the door,
The wise men entered in;
The shepherds followed after them
To hear the song begin.

And Mary held the little child
And sat upon the ground;
She looked up, she looked down,
She looked all around.

The angels sang thro' all the night
Until the rising sun,
But little Jesus fell asleep
Before the song was done.

SARA TEASDALE

THE WISE MEN ASK
THE CHILDREN THE WAY

"Dear children," they asked
    in every town,
Three kings from the land of the sun,
"Which is the road to Bethlehem?"

But neither the old nor the young
Could tell, and the kings rode on;
Their guide was a star in the air
Of gold, which glittered ahead of them,
So clear, so clear.

The star stood still over Joseph's house.
They all of them stepped in;
The good ox lowed,
    and the little child cried,
And the kings began to sing.

HEINRICH HEINE

THE SEASON OF THE STAR

This is the time of wonder,
The season of the star;
Enraptured by its splendor
Our thoughts go winging far
Across the memories and miles,
Like angel melody,
Till every face is wreathed in smiles;
Hearts hold tranquility.

And as the snow falls, pure and white,
On roof and street and hill,
Joy settles in our hearts tonight,
Glad tidings of goodwill.
On homes and hearthfires, peace descends,
And as the candles glow,
Flames of faith are kindled;
Love shines across the snow.

ALICE MacKENZIE SWAIM

THE THREE KINGS

When the star in the East was lit to shine
The three kings journeyed to Palestine;
They came from the uttermost parts of earth
With long trains laden with gifts of worth.

The first king rode on a camel's back;
He came from the land where kings are black,
Bringing treasures desired of kings,
Rubies and ivory and precious things.

An elephant carried the second king;
He came from the land of the sun-rising,
And gems and gold and spices he bare
With broidered raiment for kings to wear.

The third king came without steed or train
From the misty land where the white kings reign.
He bore no gifts save the myrrh in his hand,
For he came on foot from a far-off land.

Now when they had traveled for many days
Through tangled forests and desert ways,
By angry seas and by paths thorn-set
On Christmas Vigil the three kings met.

And over their meeting a shrouded sky
Made dark the star they had traveled by.
Then the first king spake and he frowned and said,
"By some ill spell have our feet been led.

Now I see in the darkness the fools we are
To follow the light of a lying star.
Let us fool no more but like kings and men
Each get him home to his land again!"

Then the second king with the weary face,
Gold-tint as the sun of his reigning place,
Lifted sad eyes to the clouds and said,
"It was but a dream and the dream is sped.

We dreamed of a star that rose new and fair,
But it sets in the night of the old despair.
Yet night is faithful though stars betray,
It will lead to our kingdoms far away."

God used the Old Testament prophets to prepare His people for the Messiah's birth. Christ's adoration by the Magi was foretold in the Book of Psalms: "May all kings fall down before him" (Psalm 72:11). Photo of Giza, Egypt, by Don North.

Then spake the king who had fared alone
From the far-off kingdom, the white-hung throne:
"O brothers, brothers, so very far
Ye have followed the light of the radiant star,

And because for a while ye see it not
Shall its faithful shining be all forgot?
On the spirit's pathway the light still lies
Though the star be hid from our longing eyes.

Tomorrow our star will be bright once more
The little pin-hole in heaven's floor—
The Angels pricked it to let it bring
Our feet to the throne of the new-born King!"

And the first king heard and the second heard
And their hearts grew humble before the third.
And they laid them down beside bale and beast
And their sleeping eyes saw light in the East.

For the Angels fanned them with starry wings
And the waft of visions of unseen things.
And the next gold day waned trembling and white,
And the star was born of the waxing night.

And the three kings came where the Great King lay,
A little baby among the hay.
The ox and the ass were standing near
And Mary, mother beside her Dear.

Then low in the litter the kings bowed down;
They gave Him gold for a kingly crown

And frankincense for a great God's breath
And Myrrh to sweeten the day of death.

The maiden Mother she stood and smiled,
And she took from the manger her little child.
On the dark king's head she laid His hand
And anger died at that dear command.

She laid His hand on the gold king's head
And despair itself was comforted.
But when the pale king knelt in the stall
She heard on the straw his tears down fall.

And she stooped where he knelt beside her feet
And laid on his bosom her baby sweet.
And the king in the holy stable-place
Felt the little lips through the tears on his face.

Christ! lay Thy hand on the angry king
Who reigns in my breast to my undoing,
And lay Thy hands on the king who lays
The spell of sadness on all my days,

And give the white king my soul, Thy soul,
Of these other kings the high control.
That soul and spirit and sense may meet
In adoration before Thy feet!

Now Glory to God the Father Most High
And the Star, the Spirit, He leads us by.
And to God's dear Son, the Babe who was born
And laid in the manger on Christmas morn!

EDITH BLAND NESBIT

JESUS' WORLD

As the most precious metal, gold is regarded as symbolic of what pertains to God and signifies His divine righteousness.

A *magus* was a person who interpreted dreams. Magi lived a spartan life of self-denial and were greatly respected for their knowledge and education. The term was used to mean any wise man who sought the truth.

According to John 19:39–40, after Jesus' crucifixion, His body was wrapped in linen and myrrh and aloes. Jesus received the gift of myrrh twice in His life: at His birth and at His death.

The Magi set out, probably on camels, to follow a star which they considered to be an omen. Perhaps they were aware of the prophecy about the birth of the king of the Jews, or at the very least, they thought the star signaled the birth or death of a great person. Photo of camel by Lior Rubin.

Gold has always been considered a precious metal. In the Bible, gold is first mentioned in Genesis 2:11-12.

The frankincense and myrrh which the Magi presented to Jesus were likely in their most common forms as a gum or a resin. Photo of frankincense in silver containers by Charles O. Cecil/Visuals Unlimited.

It was not until about the eighth century that names were given to the Magi. Tradition identifies them as Balthasar, Melchior, and Gaspar, kings of Arabia, Persia, and India respectively.

Myrrh comes from the leaves of the rock rose plant.

The gifts the Magi presented to the Infant were symbolic: gold represented the gift of substance, that the Child should never want for anything; frankincense, a rare fragrance, represented the peace of the inner thought; and myrrh, a rare herb of great price used in Egyptian embalming, symbolized the idea that the Child would rise above bitter disappointment to be in full agreement with God.

Sometime around the third century, the Magi were considered to be kings.

Frankincense comes from the fragrant resin of the frankincense tree. It was an ingredient in the anointing oil used in the Temple. Photo of frankincense tree by Anthony Dalton.

A Boy in Bethlehem

Olaf Ruhen

Of the night that changed the world his memory should be clear—but the boy who nestled against the neck of the lead ox is not sure he really saw all the things he remembered.

I can remember everything about that day: the wind, a light stirring of fine, sharp air; the sky pale blue, the blue sky of a fine winter day; the earth brown with winter. My father was busy with his brothers, Manasses and Eliud. They were staying with us. Because of them my father stayed home from the vineyard, and for awhile I stayed with him; but I kept thinking what a good day it would be to spend with the shepherds, and after awhile he told me to go.

After I had walked down the hill and looked over to where the shepherds were grazing their flocks on the lower slopes of the hills, I decided that the open fields would be too cold. There was a sunny corner out of the wind where old Aaron was working on his terraces. He was building rough field stones into a new wall; and I spent most of the day with him there, helping him where I could.

But the sun set early on the hillside below the village, and remembering this, I started for home. The sun was still shining strong and warm when I came to the gateway of our home. There I stopped, for nothing was as it should have been.

My elder sister was grinding barley with the little stone mill, but they had been grinding barley when I left in the morning. Barley enough for ourselves and our guests should have all been ground long before noon.

But on this day my sisters were still grinding corn; there was a strange little donkey in the yard, and there were people I had never seen before. The donkey was small and puny; my father would never have bought him. This one was tired with a long journey too; his hoofs were worn too

When the Stars of Morning Sang

When the stars of morning
   sang long ago,
Sweet the air with music rang
   through the snow;
There beside the mother mild
Slept the blessed
   Christmas Child—
Slumber holy, undefiled—
   Here below.

When the wise men traveled
   far through the night,
Following the guiding star,
   pure and bright,
Lo! it stood above the place
Sanctified by Heaven's grace,
And upon the Christ-Child's
   face shed its light.

When the world lay hushed
   and still Christmas morn,
Suddenly were skies athrill—
   "Christ is born!"
Angel voices, high and clear,
   chanted tidings of
   good cheer,
"See the Infant King is here,
   Christ is born!"

Anne P. L. Field

Donkeys, like camels, are a practical form of transportation in the hilly areas surrounding Jerusalem. People, like these Bedouins, still use these animals to traverse the dusty roads of Israel. Photo by Jeff Greenberg/Visuals Unlimited.

close; he needed a long spell on good soft pasture.

A tall man was coming from the stable. I had never seen him before, but I guessed this was my Uncle Joseph. He was tall and straight and bearded; and though he was a Nazarene he had the face of a man of the open air, as though he were a shepherd, or a worker in stone. I learned later that he was a carpenter.

"It's a poor room I have for you," my father said, but Joseph grinned cheerfully.

"We've slept in worse places, Jacob," he said. "I learned long ago to stretch my legs according to my bed."

Our meal was late, very late, and when it was over I was sent straight to a bed in the courtyard under a little dome that supported the rooms near the outer wall. I watched the stars, and I listened to the sounds: the talk from the house, the movements of cattle in the stable, and once, the tramping of a squad of Romans in the road outside. I thought I would never get to sleep; then suddenly I was wide awake and knew that I had been sleeping for hours.

It was a cry that had wakened me, I thought, and I waited a long time as though I expected another, but none came. I was wide awake, as though I had never been asleep, and I thought I had never seen a night so lovely, so crystal clear, so serene in spite of a confusion of sounds from the stable. There was movement there; I could see a flickering of lamps from deep inside, and there was a little bustle of people. I puzzled and puzzled; and then I guessed: my new cousin had been born; and I wondered whether my Uncle Joseph had been right; whether it had been a son, for that was important to him.

After awhile I couldn't lie there any longer, and when there had been no one moving for a while I got up and hurried over to the entrance to the stable. Just inside was a place where, long before, my grandfather, or perhaps his father, had begun to widen the cave. The wall had been cut deeper here; and then later masons had left a little stack of squared limestone blocks in the

LEGEND OF THE SMALLEST CAMEL

Heedless of all about him,
  and little caring
For aught except relief
  from the load he bore,
The smallest camel, tired
  from the day's hard faring,
Gladly knelt, at command,
  by the stable door.

The long night passed,
  and master and slave, together,
Slumbered as rank assigned them,
  each to his own;
But the smallest camel,
  trailing his broken tether,
Returned to watch by the door
  where a halo shone.

On the homeward trail,
  in humble reverie vested,
Old Gaspar mused as he rode
  with tightened rein,
"The little one seems
  oddly refreshed and rested—
He was tired at the journey's end,
  and I sensed his pain."

Balthasar said, "He tarried
  not with the others—
I found him again
  at the crib in the early morn;
Methinks he hastens
  but to rejoin his brothers
And boast that he knelt at the
  place where a King was born!"

DANA K. AKERS

A CHRISTMAS CAROL

They leave the land
   of gems and gold,
The shining portals
   of the East;
For Him, the woman's
   Seed foretold,
They leave the revel
   and the feast.

To earth their scepters
   they have cast,
And crowns by kings
   ancestral worn;
They track the lonely
   Syrian waste;
They kneel before the
   Babe new born.

O happy eyes that saw
   Him first,
O happy lips that kissed
   His feet
Earth slakes at last
   her ancient thirst,
With Eden's joy
   her pulses beat.

True kings are those
   who thus forsake
Their kingdoms for the
   Eternal King;
Serpent, her foot is on
   thy neck;
Herod, thou writhest,
   but canst sting.

He, He is King, and
   He alone
Who lifts that Infant hand
   to bless,
Who makes His mother's
   knee His throne
Yet rules the starry wilderness.

AUBREY DE VERE

---

cutting, where they would be in no one's way. It was a play-place of mine and I knew it well, so I watched my chance and when no one was looking, I slipped into the shadows amongst the stones where it would be hard to see me.

The oxen were lying down, chewing the cud. They knew me; it was my regular chore to take them out to graze, and I could walk all over them without them stirring. The yokes and the harness hung on the wall nearby and threw a shadow; so when I was sure that no one would see me I went up and stood there and watched.

I saw the baby. It was such a tiny little red and runty thing that I felt sorry for my uncle; it was blotched, and I was sad. I was still looking when I heard the men coming across the courtyard and walked past me to the end stall. I lay beside Speckles, our lead ox, up near his head.

My family left after awhile so that Joseph could talk to his wife. I would have gone, but there was too much risk they would see me, so I stayed; but Joseph talked quietly and I could not hear what he said. When Joseph too came out he saw me. He stopped, and I think he smiled. I could not see his expression in the dark of the cave, and I thought perhaps he was telling me to leave, and I got up. But he patted me on the crown of my head and turned me round, and sent me back to where I had come from, by Speckles' head. I think he knew I would not have cared to have my father find out I had stolen in.

All this I can remember as clearly as though it were yesterday; but from then, from the commotion at the gate that followed, it all seems like a dream, so rich and dreamlike I sometimes think I must have slept again. Yet I know I didn't; the things happened; they happened according to the prophecies, as my father has often told me, and my thinking could not change them.

And first were the travelers at the gate, three simple men dressed as travelers, but in fine cloth and armed with good blades. The three men came, walking like kings; and in the moonlit courtyard they looked like

kings, and I have since heard it said that in those far countries from which they came they ruled as kings.

They spoke to my father and his brothers, and they came into the dim lit stable. They stood a long time near the manger, and I knelt up in the straw to watch them; and I think I shall see it always: the glorious men beyond in the light: and they knelt to the new Baby, so that He seemed to take to Himself the glory that the men brought with them. The three men opened their gifts and left them on the ledge at the head of the stall, and when at last they went, the little bound figure of the Babe was surrounded with frankincense and myrrh and gifts of gold.

I came forward as they were going—I don't know why—and stood by Speckles, near his tail. The first two

Because of their ability to travel long distances with little water, camels were often used for transportation in arid regions. Camels can travel twenty-five miles a day and go three days without water. For desert dwellers, camels were a source of milk and leather and their hair was woven into tent curtains and rugs. Photo by SuperStock.

TWELFTH NIGHT: SONG OF THE CAMELS

Not born to the forest are we,
Not born to the plain,
To the grass and the
    shadowing tree
And the splashing of rain.
Only the sand we know
And the cloudless sky.
The mirage and the
    deep-sunk well
And the stars on high.

To the sound of our bells we came
With huge soft stride,
Kings riding upon our backs,
Slaves at our side.
Out of the east drawn on
By a dream and a star,
Seeking the hills and the groves
Where the fixed towns are.

Our goal was no palace gate,
No temple of old,
But a Child on His mother's lap
In the cloudy cold.
The olives were windy and white,
Dust swirled through the town,
As all in their royal robes
Our masters knelt down.

- ELIZABETH JANE COATSWORTH

men saw me and passed without saying anything, though they smiled, I think, as well as I was able to tell in the dark. But the third paused and put his hand on my shoulder, and said something to me; but he spoke in Greek, I think. I could not understand it.

They spoke in Greek to my father and his brothers, but only Joseph understood them; the others had not more than a word or two, but in Nazareth it was necessary to know the Greek tongue, for Nazareth was on the highway to Asia Minor. They spoke for a long while; then they paid their respects to my father and left.

"What did they seek?" my father asked. "What were the gifts for? How did they come here?"

"They followed a star," said Joseph. "They have followed it a long time from a strange land."

"A star?" asked Manasses. "What star?" He looked up at the heavens and all the stars were very bright.

"A star stood in the east, and they followed it," Joseph said.

"They followed it here?" my father asked. From his voice he must have been as I was; he must have felt it to be a dream.

"They followed it to Herod," Joseph said. "The star was the star of the King of the Jews; and so they followed it to Herod; and when they found Herod, they lost the star. And Herod asked the scribes what birthplace the prophets had foretold for the King of the Jews. The scribes said 'Bethlehem,' and the wise men came here."

"Without the star?" Manasses asked.

"They found it again, in a well. They found it on the road to Bethlehem. They had forgotten, they said, to watch the skies, and so it was shown to them, reflected in a well. And the star rose up and settled against the edge of the mountain, above this town of Bethlehem and above this house."

"You take this steadily, that your child should be called King of the Jews," my father said; and Joseph answered, "I have known it a long time."

A PROMISE FULFILLED

The King of Kings lay in a
lowly manger, In all our trials
born to be our friend.
He knows our need, to our
weakness is no stranger.
Behold your King!
before Him lowly bend!

JESUS AT THE TEMPLE

nd when eight days were accomplished for the circumcising of the child, his name was called JESUS, which was so named of the angel before he was conceived in the womb.

And when the days of her purification according to the law of Moses were accomplished, they brought him to Jerusalem, to present him to the Lord; (As it is written in the law of the Lord, Every male that openeth the womb shall be called holy to the Lord.) And to offer a sacrifice according to that which is said in the law of the Lord, a pair of turtledoves or two young pigeons.

And, behold, there was a man in Jerusalem, whose name was Simeon; and the same man was just and devout, waiting for the consolation of Israel: and the Holy Ghost was upon him.

And it was revealed unto him by the Holy Ghost, that he should not see death, before he had seen the Lord's Christ.

And he came by the Spirit into the temple: and when the parents brought in the child Jesus, to do for him after the custom of the law. Then took he him up in his arms, and blessed God, and said,

Lord, now lettest thou thy servant depart in peace, according to thy word: For mine eyes have seen thy salvation, which thou hast prepared before the face of all people; a light to lighten the Gentiles, and the glory of thy people Israel.

And Joseph and his mother marvelled at those things which were spoken of him.

And Simeon blessed them, and said unto Mary his mother, Behold, this child is set for the fall and rising again of many in Israel; and for a sign which shall be spoken against; (Yea, a sword shall pierce through thy own soul also,) that the thoughts of many hearts may be revealed (*Luke 2:21–35*).

Jewish law decreed that Mary and Joseph present their first-born male child to the Lord at the Temple in Jerusalem thirty-three days after His birth. In Simon Vouet's THE PRESENTATION AT THE TEMPLE (Musee du Louvre/SuperStock), Joseph holds the two pigeons required for Mary's purification. These birds were given to the priest for a burnt offering.

THE SENTINEL

FULTON J. SHEEN

imeon was like a sentinel whom God had sent to watch for the Light. When the Light finally appeared, he was ready to sing. In a poor Child brought by poor people making a poor offering, Simeon discovered the riches of the world. As this old man held the Child in his arms, he did not look back, but forward, and not only to the future of his own people but to the future of all the Gentiles of all the tribes and nations of the earth. An old man at the sunset of his own life spoke of the sunrise of the world; in the evening of life he told of the promise of a new day. He had seen the Messiah before by faith; now his eyes could close, for there was nothing more beautiful to look upon. Some flowers open only in the evening.

Simeon's hymn was an act of adoration. There are three acts of adoration described in the early life of the Divine Child. The shepherds adored; Simeon and Anna the prophetess adored; and the Magi adored. The song of Simeon was like a sunset in which a shadow heralds a substance. It was the first hymn by men in the life of Christ.

After his hymn of praise he addressed himself only to the mother; Simeon knew that she, and not Joseph, was related to the Babe in his arms. He saw furthermore that there were sorrows in store for her, not for Joseph.

It was as if the whole history of the Divine Child were passing before the eyes of the old man. Every detail of that prophecy was to be fulfilled within the lifetime of the Babe. Here was a hard fact of the Cross, affirmed even before the tiny arms of the Babe could stretch themselves out straight enough to make the form of a cross.

Joseph, Mary, and Jesus probably began their six-mile journey from Bethlehem to the Temple in Jerusalem during the cool hours of the morning in order to escape the noonday heat. Photo of Jerusalem at sunrise by Thomas R. Fletcher.

A Song for Simeon

Lord, the Roman hyacinths are blooming in bowls, and
The winter sun creeps by the snow hills;
The stubborn season has made stand.
My life is light, waiting for the death wind,
Like a feather on the back of my hand.
Dust in sunlight and memory in corners
Wait for the wind that chills towards the dead land.

Grant us Thy peace.
I have walked many years in this city,
Kept faith and fast, provided for the poor,
Have given and taken honour and ease.
There went never any rejected from my door.
Who shall remember my house, where shall live my children's children
When the time of sorrow is come?
They will take to the goat's path, and the fox's home,
Fleeing from the foreign faces and the foreign swords.

Before the time of cords and scourges and lamentation
Grant us Thy peace.
Before the stations of the mountain of desolation,
Before the certain hour of maternal sorrow,
Now at this birth season of decease,
Let the Infant, the still unspeaking and unspoken Word,
Grant Israel's consolation
To one who has eighty years and no to-morrow.

According to Thy word.
They shall praise Thee and suffer in every generation
With glory and derision,
Light upon light, mounting the saints' stair.
Not for me the martyrdom, the ecstasy of thought and prayer,
Not for me the ultimate vision.
Grant me Thy peace.
(And a sword shall pierce Thy heart,
Thine also).
I am tired with my own life and the lives of those after me,
I am dying in my own death and the deaths of those after me.
Let Thy servant depart,
Having seen Thy salvation.

T .S. Eliot

Simeon had patiently waited for the Messiah's birth and, upon seeing the infant Jesus, knew that prophecy had finally been fulfilled. In Philippe de Champaigne's Presentation in the Temple *(SuperStock), Simeon blesses God for His faithfulness toward His people.*

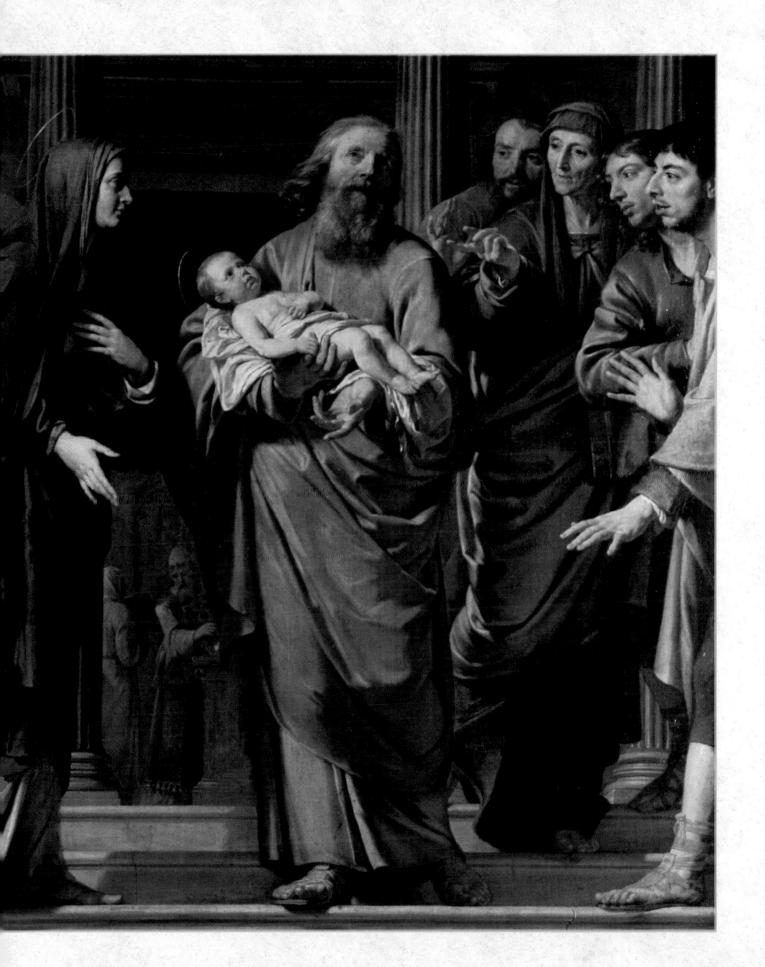

THE FLIGHT INTO EGYPT

 nd when the shepherds were departed, behold, the angel of the Lord appeareth to Joseph in a dream, saying, Arise, and take the young child and his mother, and flee into Egypt, and be thou there until I bring thee word: for Herod will seek the young child to destroy him.

When he arose, he took the young child and his mother by night, and departed into Egypt:

And was there until the death of Herod: that it might be fulfilled which was spoken of the Lord by the prophet, saying, Out of Egypt have I called my son.

Then Herod, when he saw that he was mocked of the wise men, was exceeding wroth, and sent forth and slew all the children that were in Bethlehem, and in all the coasts thereof, from two years old and under, according to the time which he had diligently enquired of the wise men. Then was fulfilled that which was spoken by Jeremy the prophet, saying, In Rama was there a voice heard, lamentation, and weeping, and great mourning, Rachel weeping for her children, and could not be comforted, because thy are not (*Matthew 2: 13–18*).

The angels guide Joseph, Mary, and Jesus in THE FLIGHT INTO EGYPT *by Jacob Jordeans (Christie's Images/Super-Stock). In order to avoid Herod's edict that every male child under two be killed, the family left Bethlehem at night, making its way into Egypt, like the children of Israel during the Exodus. Jesus left Israel for Egypt, only to be called back to fulfill God's promise.*

ALL THE ROAD TO EGYPT

All the road to Egypt
Sang to see them pass,
The Child asleep on Mary's arm,
Old Joseph shielding them from harm,
The Angel, beautiful as hope,
Leading by a twist of rope
The little, gray-coat ass.

All the road to Egypt
Knelt to see them pass,
The Child's dear head haloed gold,
Madonna's robe in many a fold
Of changing blue like shimmering wave,
Whose falling grace a glory gave
Even to the dusty ass.

All the road to Egypt
Danced to see them pass,
Old Joseph's cloak of cinnamon,
The Angel's restless wings that shone
Green as the trees of Paradise,
And like some curious, chased device
A little silver ass.

All the road to Egypt
Bloomed to feel them pass;
So raced the sap in stem and root,
The withered fig tree sprang to fruit;
The palm and olive bowed their load
To Mary's lips; that purple road
Bore thistles for the ass.

KATHARINE LEE BATES

THE FLIGHT INTO EGYPT

Out of the land of Judaea
Where wise men had followed the star,
Out of a birthplace so humble
They fled to find safety afar.

Into the night, mysterious,
They hurried past desert and stream
To dwell for a time with strangers,
For they had been warned in a dream.

Simple their trust, unquestioned,
That the Child who was placed in their care
Was destined to become the Saviour
Of men of goodwill everywhere.

Out of the past spoke the prophet
From writings both sacred and old.
The one who had promised a Saviour,
This flight into Egypt foretold.

ALICE LEEDY MASON

The mighty pyramids of the Nile River delta still stand much as they did when Joseph, Mary, and Jesus journeyed into Egypt. The family may have followed in the footsteps of Abraham, who also escaped into Egypt. Photo of pyramids by SuperStock.

BORNE TO SAFETY

HENRY DANIEL-ROPS

n angel of the Lord appeared to Joseph and said: "Arise and take the young child and mother and flee into Egypt and be thou there until I send thee word: for Herod will seek the young child to destroy him." Joseph set out that very night for Egypt where, ever since the destruction of Jerusalem by Nebuchadnezzar, there had been a considerable Jewish colony which had continued to expand after Palestine became a Greek province, until it became nearly a million strong. Jewish colonists had even built at Leontopolis a temple said to rival that of Zion. The majority of these Jews remained faithful to Palestine and in constant relations with their compatriots there. It was natural that if Joseph had to flee from Palestine he should go to Egypt.

So the family set off with the Child. The ass bore all the belongings and all the hopes of these poor people, the good faithful beast plodding along by stages of about thirty miles. They would probably follow the caravan route which hugged the coast as closely as possible, for the interior of the country was frightful, a vast waste of barren sand without the meanest vegetation except on the borders where a thin, stony soil supported a scanty growth.

We know nothing about the sojourn in Egypt, but it could not have been very long, for Matthew tells us that being told of Herod's death by the angel, Joseph took Mary and Jesus back to Palestine. But hearing that Archelaus had succeeded his father, Herod, Joseph did not venture in Judea but returned to Galilee. Most likely, Jesus was somewhere between eight months and eighteen months old when his parents returned to their native land.

Joseph, Mary, and Jesus undoubtedly crossed into Egypt by the shortest and quickest route. The family may have seen architectural wonders similar to Nicolas Poussin's rendering of THE REST ON THE FLIGHT TO EGYPT (Hermitage Museum/Bridgeman Art Library, London/SuperStock). The upper Nile delta was a bustling center of trade and commerce.

JESUS' WORLD

According to Jewish laws, Mary was required to present herself at the Temple in Jerusalem for purification after Christ's birth. At this time she would also present Jesus to the Lord, as was the law for all first-born sons.

Scholars estimate that Herod the Great died in 4 B.C. and date Jesus' birth between one to three years before the ruler's death.

The floors of ancient homes in Nazareth consisted of a solidly packed mixture of dirt, clay, and ash.

Joseph, Mary, and Jesus may have traveled from Egypt to Bethlehem on a Roman road named "The Way of the Sea."

Egypt had long attracted refugees because of its proximity to the arid land of Canaan, its climate, and its way of life. Photo of acacia tree in the Egyptian desert by Richard T. Nowitz.

During times of crises, many of God's people left Israel for Egypt. Abraham took his family to Egypt during a famine. Jacob and his sons also went to Egypt during a famine. Jeroboam escaped King Solomon's wrath by fleeing to Egypt. Later, the prophet Jeremiah also sought refuge there.

Joseph, Mary, and Jesus may have spent up to three years in Egypt.

Jesus' presentation at the Temple was in accordance with the law God gave to Moses that all first-born children be presented to the Lord. The Lord said to Moses, "Sanctify unto me all the first-born, whatsoever openeth the womb among the children of Israel . . . it is mine" (*Exodus 13:2*).

Nazareth was a small village of perhaps no more than one-hundred people. Photo of Nazareth by Thomas R. Fletcher.

The purification ceremony marked an end to the ritual restrictions that accompanied childbirth. Usually a lamb was sacrificed to God in this ceremony, but less wealthy people offered birds, such as doves or pigeons. Photo of doves by Tom Edwards/Visuals Unlimited.

Like many people of the time, Joseph and Mary probably lived in a square, flat-roofed, one-room house, built of dried-mud bricks. The exterior of most houses were painted white, and the interior was left its natural brick color.

Typical furnishings of the time consisted of floor mats, stools, and a single small, low wooden table.

THE RETURN TO NAZARETH

ut when Herod was dead, behold, an angel of the Lord appeareth in a dream to Joseph in Egypt, saying, Arise, and take the young child and his mother, and go into the land of Israel: for they are dead which sought the young child's life.

And he arose, and took the young child and his mother, and came into the land of Israel. But when he heard that Archelaus did reign in Judaea in the room of his father Herod, he was afraid to go thither: notwithstanding, being warned of God in a dream, he turned aside into the parts of Galilee:

And he came and dwelt in a city called Nazareth: that it might be fulfilled which was spoken by the prophets, He shall be called a Nazarene (*Matthew 2:19–23*).

This portrayal of Joseph, Mary, and Jesus in THE RETURN FROM EGYPT (Christie's Images/SuperStock) by an unknown artist depicts their journey back to Israel. Egypt was a place of refuge, but Nazareth was home. According to Matthew, being a Nazarene also fulfilled Messianic prophecy. Although we know little of Jesus' childhood, we can assume He was brought up in a household where He learned Joseph's carpentry skills and studied the Old Testament. When Jesus was twelve years old He amazed the scholars in the Temple by His understanding and His answers to their questions.

HOME AGAIN TO NAZARETH

HENRY VAN DYKE

ever in his life had Joseph been so well-off for money as he was after the visit of the wise men. It was not vast wealth they brought him, but it was enough to make him easy in mind and hopeful for the future.

First, there were the rare and precious gums of frankincense and myrrh, the surplus of which could be sold for a considerable sum. Second, there was the gold, not a huge quantity, but at least a tribute worthy to be presented by princes to the Prince. With this small capital in hand, Joseph could set himself up in his trade and stay on as a carpenter in Bethlehem. This idea appealed to him strongly, for Bethlehem was a pleasant place in a fertile region. He had made friends there, and it was near the Temple.

"There are two carpenters here already," said he, "but there is room and need for another. The town is growing. We are right on the road from Jerusalem to Egypt; the caravans pass. They give a lot of work in repairs on pack-saddles and chariots. I know of a good place for a work-shop."

Mary was silent. She was thinking of the dear, white little house in Nazareth, the silvery olive-trees in the small garden, the flowing spring under its stone arch, and the friendly peace of the hills and vales of Galilee.

Did not the rabbis say that Galilee was a better place than Judea to bring up a child? Was not that her first and dearest duty, the holy charge given to her bands? Yet she would do what her husband wanted; stay with him here in Bethlehem or go with him anywhere in the world.

Joseph slept, and another dream came to him, a strange sudden dream, disquieting, full of alarm. They were great dreamers in those times, and they paid attention to their visions.

HOME TO NAZARETH

Coarse, harsh cloth for His
    swaddling clothes
And rough-stemmed hay
    for the Christ-Child's bed
And the only lamp, a star
    that shone
Through the rafters overhead.

But Mary pillowed the
    little form
On an arm as soft as a white
    dove's breast,
And she shaped the hay
    with her gentle hands
Into a soft downy nest.

And she thought of a room
    in Nazareth,
Of a white bed under the
    eaves of sod—
Strange that she should have
    given birth
Here to the Son of God.

Strange these coarse, harsh
    swaddling clothes
On the tender flesh of her
    little One,
When there were robes in a
    cedar chest,
Cedar from Lebanon.

"I will take Thee home, my
    little Son,"
Mary, the beautiful
    mother, said,
"I will take Thee home to my
    small, clean room,
Home to a soft, clean bed.

"And I will open a
    fragrant chest
Which Joseph, Thy father,
    hath made.
In it are fine, twilled
    linen slips,
And a woolly coat is laid.

"Fine, twilled linen from
    silver flax,
And fleecy wool from a snow-
    white sheep—
Yea, we will go home
    through the starry dusk.
Sleep, my little One, sleep."

GRACE NOLL CROWELL

This new dream was terrifying.

An angel told of Herod's design to have all the infant boys in Bethlehem killed by his soldiers, hoping thus to destroy the young Child whom he feared and hated as his rival for the throne. It was a madman's idea, unspeakably cruel. Joseph was numb with the terror of his dream.

"Get up," said the angel, "and take the young Child and His mother, and flee into Egypt, and stay there until I tell thee."

Joseph rose quickly, and told Mary the strange message that had come to him. With part of his gold he bought a strong white ass of the famous breed of the Nile and gear for the journey. Hasty were the preparations and the farewells.

Dark was the night when the family took the great south road for the distant land of the Sphinx and the Pyramids, the land where the children of Israel were once in bondage and where the ancient idols were still throned in their crumbling temples.

The Child who was born to overthrow them had no throne but His mother's breast. There He reigned, in peace and joy, while the strong ass bore them through the darkness towards exile and safety. It was the longest journey that Jesus ever took on earth.

What befell them in Egypt, and what they saw there, we do not know and cannot guess. What is certain is that the family stayed there until the wicked Herod died of a loathsome disease, and his son Archelaus reigned over Judea. Then Joseph made up his mind that it would be safe to go back to Judea and set up that new carpenter shop which he had planned.

But it was not to be so.

Another dream came to him in which he was warned not to return to Bethlehem but to go straight on to his old home in Galilee.

Mary came again to the little gray house that she loved and the carpenter-shop in Nazareth. There it was that the thought of Jesus had first entered Mary's heart. There the Boy lived and was obedient to His parents and grew strong, filled with wisdom.

O HOLY NIGHT

O Holy night, the stars are brightly shining;
It is the night of the dear Saviour's birth.
Long lay the world in sin and error pining,
Till He appeared and the soul felt its worth.
A thrill of hope the weary world rejoices,
For yonder breaks a new and glorious morn;
Fall on your knees,
Oh hear the angel voices!
O night divine, O night when Christ was born!
O night, O holy night, O night divine!

Led by the light of faith serenely beaming,
With glowing hearts by His cradle we stand.
So led by light of a star sweetly gleaming,
Here came the wise men from the Orient land.
The King of Kings lay in a lowly manger,
In all our trials born to be our friend.
He knows our need,
To our weakness is no stranger.
Behold your King! before Him lowly bend!
Behold your King! your King! before Him bend!

Truly He taught us to love one another;
His law is love, and His gospel is peace.
Chains shall He break, for the slave is our brother,
And in His name all oppression shall cease.
Sweet hymns of joy in grateful chorus praise we;
Let all within us praise His holy name.
Christ is the Lord!
Then ever, ever raise we;
His power and glory evermore proclaim!
His power and glory evermore proclaim!

ADOLPHE CHARLES ADAM

THE HOLY LAND AT CHRIST'S BIRTH

- - - - Marks the probable route from Nazareth to Bethlehem that Joseph and Mary traveled. Jesus was born in Bethlehem.

.... Marks the probable route from the East to Bethlehem that the Magi traveled in order to present Jesus with gifts of gold, frankinsense, and myrrh.

- - - - Marks the probable route from Bethlehem to Egypt that Joseph, Mary, and Jesus traveled when an angel of the Lord told Joseph to flee Israel.

- - - - Marks the probable route from Egypt to Nazareth that Joseph, Mary, and Jesus took after the angel of the Lord told Joseph to return to Israel. The family avoided the territory controlled by Herod's son, Archelaus, and followed the Mediterranean coastline.

GALILEE

Nazareth

Sea of Galilee

Jordan River

JUDEA

Jerusalem

Bethlehem

GREAT SEA (MEDITERRANEAN SEA)

Salt Sea (Dead Sea)

SINAI

EGYPT

Gulf of Suez

INDEX
of
titles and authors

ACKNOWLEDGMENTS (CONTINUED FROM PAGE 4)

Eliot, T. S. "A Song for Simeon" from COLLECTED POEMS 1909-1962 by T. S. Eliot, copyright 1936 by Harcourt, Inc., copyright © 1964, 1963 by T. S. Eliot, reprinted by permission of the publisher. Goudge, Elizabeth. "Michael and the Shepherd" from THE WELL OF THE STAR. Reprinted by permission of Harold Ober Associates Incorporated, copyright 1941 by Elizabeth Goudge. Holmes, Marjorie. Excerpt from THREE FROM GALILEE, © 1972, 1986 by Marjorie Holmes. Reprinted by permission of the author. Nicholson, Martha Snell. "And His Name Shall Be Called Wonderful" from BEAUTIFUL POEMS ON JESUS, Basil Miller (Comp.), Kansas City, MO, Beacon Hill Press, © 1948. Olson, Richard P. "The Three Strangers" from THE PRACTICAL DREAMER AND OTHER STORIES TO TELL AT CHRISTMAS. Copyright © 1990 by Richard P. Olson. Used by permission of Upper Room Books. Oursler, Fulton. "Blessed Among Women" and "Shepherds at the Back Door" from THE GREATEST STORY EVER TOLD by Fulton Oursler. Copyright 1949 by Fulton Oursler. Used by permission of Doubleday, a division of Random House, Inc. Peck, Katherine Blackburn. "The Carpenter's Son" from BEAUTIFUL POEMS ON JESUS, Basil Miller (Comp), Kansas City, MO, Beacon Hill Press, © 1948. Roberts, Jenny. "Bethlehem" from THE BIBLE THEN AND NOW, copyright 1996 by Quarto Inc. Ruhen, Olaf. "A Boy In Bethlehem." Reprinted by permission of The Saturday Evening Post, 1958. Sheen, Fulton J. Excerpts from LIFE OF CHRIST by Bishop Fulton J. Sheen. Reprinted by permission of Propagation of the Faith. Van Dyke, Henry. Excerpt from "Even Unto Bethlehem" from THE STORY OF CHRISTMAS by Henry Van Dyke. Reprinted with the permission of Scribner, a Division of Simon & Schuster. Copyright 1928 by Charles Scribner's Sons, renewed 1956. Our sincere thanks to the following authors whom we were unable to locate: Dana K. Akers for "Legend of the Smallest Camel," Sholem Asch for an excerpt from MARY, Alice Darton for an excerpt from HIS MOTHER, John Duffy for "The Annunciation," Calvin Le Compte for "The Visitation," Madeleine Sweeny Miller for "How Far to Bethlehem," Denis O'Shea for "Angels and Shepherds," M. Paulinus for "Here at the Stable Door," Father Prat for "The Betrothal," and Wolfgang Trilling for "A Name Filled With Hope."

ADDITIONAL ART CREDITS

Page 2: Lorenzo di Credi, detail of THE ANNUNCIATION (Galleria Degli Uffizi/SuperStock); Pages 6–7: Michelangelo Buonarroti, GOD DIVIDING THE WATERS AND EARTH (Sistine Chapel/SuperStock); Pages 28–29: Peitro Vannucci Perugino, THE MARRIAGE OF THE VIRGIN (Musee des Beaux-Arts/SuperStock); Pages 56-57: Hugo Van der Goes, MARY AND JOSEPH (Galleria Degli Uffizi/SuperStock); Pages 76–77: Giorgio Giorgione, ADO-RATION OF THE SHEPHERDS (National Gallery of Art/SuperStock); Pages 96–97: Charles Le Brun, ADORATION OF THE SHEPHERDS (Louvre/Art Resource); Pages 116–117: Camillo Procaccini, ADORATION OF THE MAGI (Pinacoteac di Brera/SuperStock); Pages 136–137: Luca Giordano, THE FLIGHT INTO EGYPT (Christie's Images/SuperStock); Page 156: Zefa-U.K./H. Armstrong Roberts.